I0568366

A Relational Trinity of Kindness

Relational: the way entities are interconnected and have relevance to one another. In the biblical message, God, Jesus, and Spirit are interrelated as One in the experience of loving kindness; and this is the trinity.

Dwayne Cole

ppbooks
a good word company

Parson's Porch Books

A Relational Trinity of Kindness
ISBN: Softcover 978-1-955581-56-1
Copyright © 2015 by Dwayne Cole

To order additional copies of this book, contact:

Parson's Porch Books
1-423-475-7308
www.parsonsporch.com

Parson's Porch Books is an imprint of Parson's Porch & Company (PP&C) in Cleveland, Tennessee. PP&C is an innovative non-profit organization which raises money by publishing books of noted authors, representing all genres. All donations from contributors and profits from publishing are shared with the poor.

A Relational Trinity of Kindness

Contents

PREFACE

Life is all about relationships with special people: mother, father, wife, husband, son, daughter, grandchild, relatives, and friends. Think about how these relationships give meaning and purpose to your life and make you feel all warm and loved. All of these relationships thrive on kindness. We remember people who are kind to us. This book, *A Relational Trinity of Kindness*, is about special relationships with God revealed in Jesus and present in our lives with spiritual transforming love energies. These relationships are spoken of in the Bible in many mysterious and awe inspiring ways.

You might be feeling, "I understand relationships, but why use the word Trinity?" Soon after the Bible was written church leaders coined the non-biblical word, trinity, as a way of explaining special relationships with God. It is questionable, however, whether the word has served the church well or whether it has created confusion and misunderstanding. This book is a doctrine of the trinity that seeks fresh language to mark a new path through this maze.

From my experience I have found that the word, kindness, is the best word to use for understanding these special relational ways of God. I learned that God is kind, first from the way my parents related to me and then from the gentle teachings and actions of Jesus found in the Gospels of the New Testament. In my seminary graduate studies I translated from Greek each of the Gospels, holding each word of the tender teachings of Jesus in my hands and heart. Many of those key words for kindness are treated in chapter two of this book. These Spirit inspired words have always spoken to me and encouraged me to be a better person.

In making kindness my hermeneutic for interpreting the trinity and all the scriptures, some may feel that I am packing too much meaning in this one word, kindness. In my linguistic studies I have found that words do not have meaning, they have usage. Context determines how a word is used and what its meaning should be. For example, the word, bank, has many usages. If I say that I am taking a check to the bank, it has a clear meaning by the context in which I use it. If I say that he is fishing on the river bank, bank has a different meaning. If I say she made a perfect bank shot, bank has another usage and meaning. Please hold this idea that words have usage in your memory bank as you read this book!

My use of the word kindness broadens with each successive chapter. So, I ask you to reserve judgment until you have gone with me on this adventurous journey into the mystery of God's relational ways. The adventure belongs to the adventurous, and I hope you will feel my excitement as you are reading this book.

The art on the front cover was conceived as a result of living in Alaska and viewing the Aurora Borealis or Northern Lights as this phenomenon is commonly called. For me the swirling colorful lights represent God's creative activity and the triangular points, God, Jesus, Spirit, are all about relational kindness. I suggested the Aurora lights and the triangular points of kindness to my publisher, Dr. David Russell Tullock, at Parson's Porch & Company; and he produced the cover art.

INTRODUCTION

We cannot solve old theological problems by continuing to use the same language that created the problems in the first place. Perhaps, the church, like a crustacean, needs to shed its theological skin every few years, so that it may grow a new one. This book using new language for the relational aspects of the trinity is a fresh approach to an ancient doctrine, linking the biblical concept of kindness, a central relational term, to a process oriented theology for interpreting how God is present in the world and in us in transforming tender ways.

-Dwayne Cole

Historically Christians have had difficulty understanding and explaining how God, clothed in mystery, is present in the world and in our lives. The confusion is partly rooted in the diversity of the biblical accounts that span more than a thousand years of religious history. The many different inspired authors of scripture wrote from their own perspective and historical era.[1] Compounding the problem is that each person interprets the Bible from his/her own world-view and life experiences. The biblical writers, though very diverse, do present a unity in the midst of diversity. Both the Old Testament and the New Testament affirm that God is one. Monotheism is a unifying theme of the Bible.

---

[1] See my book, *The Story of the Bible: Authority, Inspiration, Canonization, and Translation* for an understanding of how the Bible came to be.

The life and teachings of Jesus present a fresh way of seeing God, the world, and God's people. As we read the Gospels we hear Jesus saying, "You know that you have been taught, 'an eye for an eye and a tooth for a tooth.' But I tell you not to try to get even with a person who has done something to you."[2] "You have heard people say, 'love your neighbors and hate your enemies.' But I tell you to love your enemies and pray for anyone who mistreats you."[3] Jesus also said, "Don't suppose that I came to do away with the law and the prophets. I did not come to do away with them, but to give them their full meaning."[4] These sayings show that Jesus had the freedom to interpret and change his sacred scriptures, even though this was part of the conflict he constantly had with the Jewish religious leaders.

The very names, Old Testament and New Testament imply that the New Testament writers give a fresh revelation of the way God is perceived. Revelation is not static, yet this does not imply a linear progression that improves with each passing generation. Each biblical writer in all parts of the Bible struggles and has high and low moments in speaking of the mystery of God. The Old Testament revelation is complete in the sense that it was God's special revelation for God's covenant people at that particular time in their history. Christians can affirm this with the Jewish faith and still hold up our belief in a special revelation found in the

---

[2] Matthew 5:38-39. CEV.

[3] Matthew 5:43-44. CEV.

[4] Matthew 5:17. CEV.

life and teachings of Jesus made possible by his unique response to the call of God.

In teaching and preaching the gentle teachings of Jesus in my ministry for over fifty years I felt their energy and transforming power that changed lives. I sometimes struggled, like the biblical writers, to find the right word for each situation. Sometimes I ended up having to eat my words spoken in haste, and I found that a kind word seldom failed to speak to people in their time of need and left a better taste in everyone's mouth.

Seeing and feeling the tender presence of God in the world, in their sacred scriptures (our Old Testament), in Jesus' gentle teachings, and in the Spirit filled ministry of Jesus' followers, compelled the New Testament writers to find ways to understand God's relational presence in their lives and their communities. Feeling these love energies the writers gave God, Jesus, and Spirit the name, kindness.[5]

Seeking a word to unify the relational aspects of God felt in Jesus and Spirit, Tertullian (160-220 C. E.) is credited with coining the Latin word, trinitas, trinity in English. A little before Tertullian, Theophilus used the Greek term, triad, to serve the same need. Attempts to speak of the way God is known continued among other church leaders. These early attempts to state the relational truths of God were formally

---

[5] Throughout this book Spirit will be used without the article except where quoting scripture or the creeds of the church. Spirit is used as a name for God or for Jesus as risen, and context will determine the reference.

rounded out in the church councils by the fourth century of the Christian era.

Christian theologians have had difficulty with the term, trinity, from the beginning, and it has not served the church very well. For the average person in the church pew, the word, trinity, evokes the image of three Gods: Father, Son, and Holy Spirit. The Bible never intended this belief in three Gods. The one non-negotiable tenet for the Bible is **monotheism**, the belief in one God. The Shema, the central creed of both The Old and New Testaments, is this:

> *"The Lord our God is the only true God! So love the Lord your God with all your heart, soul, and strength."*[6]
> (Deuteronomy 6:4-5, CEV)

Perhaps, it is the sense of mystery surrounding these relational experiences of God's presence that propelled the search to go forward. As discussion of the trinity proceeded, the words "persons" and even "three persons" were added and ranked as the first, second, and third persons of the Godhead. A quote attributed to Tertullian, "Out of the frying pan into the fire," is appropriate for the debate that ensued. For many this language of three persons continued

---

[6] Jesus made this Old Testament commandment the basis of his New Commandment, adding the one word, mind. Jesus had the freedom to change his sacred scriptures.

to fuel the belief in three distinct Gods. Christian hymns and sermons further taught and cemented this belief that the biblical writers never intended.

The purpose of this book is not to retell the history of the trinity; but to present the word, kindness, as a rich new metaphor for understanding the relational purpose of the trinity.[7] I will seek to show how kindness is a theme throughout the scriptures, and that the biblical writers gave the name, kindness, to God, to Jesus, and to Spirit. To be sure, the kind spirit of the biblical writers was often in tension with feelings of anger, wrath, hate, and vengeance. These human negative emotions were fueled in times of captivity and intense persecution and often attributed to God.

The wrath of God is a major theme in the early chapters of the Apostle Paul's letter to the Romans, and perhaps this is a legitimate emotion when love is spurned and rejected. Wrath in Romans is affective and not effective, a feeling and not an action. God's wrath seeks change, redemption, and justice for the oppressed. God's wrath is always under the control of kindness. When I use the word, kindness, I am speaking of a tough tenderness that is merciful, gracious,

---

[7] For a brief history of the trinity and a broad listing of the types see John Cobb's chapter in *Trinity in Process: A Relational Theology of God.* Edited by Joseph A. Bracken, S. J. and Marjorie Hewitt Suchocki. New York: The Continuum Publishing Co., 1997. This is an excellent discussion of trinity by nine different process philosophy scholars.

and filled with love. Jesus displayed a tough tenderness with his critics and even with his own disciples.

My parents were kind and gentle persons, but to manage a family with thirteen children required a **tough tenderness.** Yet, it was never abusive or wrathful; it was a tenderness that graciously sought the very best for each family member. My faith is that God always seeks the very best for every person, meeting each occasion of our lives with tenderness and gently luring us to become our very best self. Loving kindness was the one unifying energy that held our family together as one. **In making kindness my principle for interpreting the relational ways of God seen in Jesus and Spirit, I am building on the unifying energy I experience in kindness.**

The non-biblical word, trinity, is a useful metaphor, if it is used as a word to represent how God relates to the world and to humans in tender saving ways. Metaphor comes from two Greek words: μετα, meaning "across," and φερος, meaning "to carry." So, a metaphor "carries across" meaning from one realm to the other, meaning that is not readily accessible to our everyday experience and understanding. The very fact that we are dealing with mystery when we talk about God is the reason we need metaphors. It is the nature of metaphor each time it is handled to present new meanings and to invite creative thinking that is often hard to put into words.

The word, kindness, as used in the title of this book, is a good trinitarian metaphor when used as a multifaceted archetypical-like biblical concept.[8] The Jungian idea of archetype is helpful for me in understanding kindness and seeing the healing power of kindness. The word, kindness, is found in almost all cultures and religions. After the destruction of the Temple in Jerusalem, Rabbi Yohannan said to Rabbi Joshua, "My son, don't grieve. We have another atonement that is as effective as (the temple). And what is it? It is acts of loving kindness."[9] The Dali Lama has said that kindness is a key concept in Buddhism. Buddha often said, "Kindness is my religion." New brain research is showing that kindness may even be grounded in evolution, as animals are tender and protective with their young.

Carl Gustaf Jung, found his archetypes in fairy tales and myths that harken back to remotest times. In Jung's practice as a medical psychiatrist he linked myth and fairytale to therapy and healing. Archetype was a way of bringing these elements together in a unity. As found in powerful time honored stories and myths, the archetype contains transformative healing energy. For me, kindness as an archetype opens avenues of healing.

This linkage of story and healing can be seen in the gentle teachings of Jesus that I gather in the theme of kindness. Jesus was a master story teller who shared deep relational truths about God through simple parables like the lost coin,

---

[8] I am using kindness as some use Sophia or wisdom or logos to name the creative, redemptive, and sanctifying work of God, all traditional Trinitarian themes. Kindness is a strong biblical term that names these relational ways of God.

[9] Aboth de Rabba Nathan, Version A, 6.

the lost sheep, and the lost son in the Gospel of Luke, chapter 15. These parable stories tell us that God is always searching for the lost, and when they are found God is as kind as a good shepherd and as forgiving as the waiting father of the prodigal.

I am making kindness modeled in the gentle teachings of Jesus as my hermeneutic for interpreting the relational truths of the trinity, as well as the whole Bible. This is my hermeneutic from Alpha to Omega, from beginning to end. The kindness of Jesus, the morning star, shines throughout the New Testament; and that kindness, as a rich relational term, has transforming energy. Here is the heartbeat of my hermeneutic, my interpretive principle, for understanding trinitarian truths:

> The kindness we show to ourselves, our family, and to all living things is the greatest healing force in the world.

In showing how God relates to the people of God, kindness fulfills one of the essentials of trinitarian language: how it affects personal transformation. Kindness is also strongly biblical and liturgical. My use of kindness as a trinitarian metaphor is grounded in biblical revelation of God. Kindness expresses this revelation best; and as a healing metaphor, in the Jungian sense, kindness is creative, redemptive, and sanctifying, all biblical themes that have often been associated with the doctrine of the trinity.[10]

Kindness as a key metaphor for the way the Jewish people experienced God, joins kindness with revelation, reason, and metaphysics. Exodus 33:19 defines God as kindness in this foundational "I am" saying. "I am God, and I show mercy and kindness to anyone I choose."[11] This verse names God as Kindness. So what the Christian belief in the trinity names as God the Father is best conceived as "God is kind." Kindness is a gender neutral term and does not alienate some people like the masculine name and sometimes an abusive name, Father.[12] The faith of Israel can

---

[10] Theologians, especially process theologians, struggle with whether Whitehead's metaphysics or biblical revelation shapes their understanding of the trinity. While I find process philosophy to be helpful in understanding the Bible, my first and greatest inspiration comes from the Bible, especially the gentle teachings of Jesus.

[11] This translation is from the *Contemporary English Version* of the American Bible Society. When translating the Hebrew and Greek words most often rendered as graciousness or grace, the CEV shows a preference for kindness. My own study of the words from classical Greek, through the Hebrew of the Old Testament and the Greek of the New Testament shows that the CEV is justified in using the word Kindness.

[12] If I speak of God as Father in sermons or prayers, I usually also use Mother or Parent. A prayer may begin like this: "Loving God, I am grateful that I have come to know you to be like a kind Father and nurturing Mother." I also use Sophia, wisdom, as an address for God. Interspersing Mother and Sophia in our sermons and prayers is a good practice to correct sexist language. Balance is needed. Yet, to substitute Mother for Father or Sophia for Jesus or Spirit in trinitarian statements would open one to the charge of substituting one sexist title for another. Women might rightly respond, "Well, we will use Mother and Sophia for the next 2000 years and then use a gender neutral term." My use of kindness as a trinitarian metaphor seeks to use a non-sexist term that is all inclusive.

be stated in these three words: God is kind. The Psalms of Israel are filled with the "loving kindness" of God. This first part of the trinity can be stated as "I believe God is kind to all living things." Kindness as a description of God moves kindness into ontology (nature of God) and metaphysics (branch of ontology, using words about of God). I am using kindness in this metaphysical sense when I say God is kind. I am also using kindness as an umbrella type term that gathers other words like love and mercy into its reach.

Kindness is also an appropriate metaphor for expressing what is intended in the second part of the Christian trinity: the Son. Whitehead often wrote of the tender element in the teachings of Jesus as expressing the essence of Christianity and having persuasive influence: "There can be no doubt as to what elements in the record have evoked a response from all that is best in human nature. The Mother, the Child, and the bare manger: the lowly man, homeless and self-forgetful, with his message of peace, love, and sympathy: the suffering, the agony, the tender words as life ebbed, the final despair: and the whole with the authority of supreme victory."[13]

The New Testament was more concerned to show the humanity of Jesus than his divinity. The Gospel of Matthew traces Jesus' lineage through Joseph.[14] Also in Matthew the people of Nazareth, Jesus' neighbors and friends, called

---

[13] Whitehead, *Adventure of Ideas.* p.167.

[14] Matthew 1:1-17.

Jesus the son of Joseph.[15] Paul expressed the birth of Jesus in these simple words: "When the time was right, God sent his Son, and a woman gave birth to him."[16] In a letter to Titus, a co-worker, Paul added these words, "When the goodness and loving kindness of God our Savior appeared, God saved us."[17] Jesus' self-designation was "I am kind." Self- designations should carry more importance than titles we apply to Jesus. The second part of the Trinity can be stated as "I believe Jesus is kind, and calls us to be kind to others."

Kindness is an especially friendly metaphor for carrying the meaning of the third aspect of the trinity: the role of Spirit. Since this part of the trinity flows from the central belief in Jesus, it is important to let Jesus define Spirit for us. Jesus virtually equates Spirit with his continuing teaching ministry. In the upper room discourses of John's Gospel we have this eternal legacy from Jesus: "I will not leave you like orphans. I will come back to you."[18] Is Jesus saying, "I will come back to you in a new spiritual sense, no longer limited by time and space?" This seems to be the meaning of the verse: "The Spirit will teach you everything and will remind you of what I said while I was with you."[19]

---

[15] Matthew 13:55.

[16] Galatians 4:4.

[17] Titus 3:4.

[18] John 14:18.

[19] John 14:26, CEV. I am using Spirit as a name for God and as a name for Jesus as a continuing Spiritual presence...

When discussing God, Jesus, and Spirit we are talking about mystery filled relationships. Using kindness as a metaphor makes these relationships as clear as possible. Kindness certainly communicates better with children than the title, Holy Spirit or Holy Ghost, which can be a spooky title to a young child. In this book, the name, Spirit, is equated either with God or with the Risen Jesus; and this is determined by context. The third part of the Trinity can be stated as "I believe the Spirit is the Risen Jesus continuing his kind teachings in the church and in the world."[20]

Using kindness as a unifying trinitarian metaphor as I have done preserves the monotheism of the Bible and at the same time shows how God relates to us in redeeming and sanctifying ways in the historical Jesus and the Risen Jesus as Spirit.[21]

Jung found many of his archetypes in fairytales. Let me illustrate kindness with the fairytale of the "Lion and the Mouse." One day a lion was enjoying a nap in the warm sunshine. A busy little mouse was looking for berries. Spotting some too high to reach she climbed on what she thought was a rock in order to reach the berries. The mouse

---

[20] Using Spirit as a name for God and a name for the Risen Jesus is closer to a binity/binitarian than trinity/trinitarian. However this book is not concerned with the history of the trinity or the historical formation of the creeds. That history is well reported. I am strictly using Kindness as a unifying metaphor for showing the relational aspects of the trinity.

[21] Chapter 2 will speak to the way God is revealed in Jesus and chapter 3 will show how the Spirit is another name for God and for the Risen Jesus.

discovered that she had not climbed on a rock, but right on a lion's head!

The lion woke with a loud roar, saying, "who dares to wake me from my nice nap?" The little mouse jumped down and tried to run away, but the lion grabbed her in his giant paw. "Oh, please," said the mouse, "do not harm me. I was only trying to reach some berries. If you spare me, I will be able to help you some day." The lion only laughed and said, "How can you, a little mouse, help the king of the jungle? That is so funny. I will let you go this time."

One day the lion got caught in a snare of strong ropes set by hunters. Unable to free himself, he roared for help. The little mouse heard the roar and felt sorry for the lion, and she ran to help him. When she found the lion, he said, "These ropes are very strong and I cannot get free." "I have an idea," said the mouse. She quickly began chewing through the thick rope with her sharp teeth. She worked hard and long and eventually freed the lion from the trap. Because of their kindness to one another, the lion and the mouse became great friends. Whether they come from myth, fairy tales, or the Bible, stories are powerful tools for teaching relational truths like kindness.[22] Old and New Testament stories profess that "The Lord our God is One." This is the one non-negotiable truth in any discussion of the trinity. The Christian Church has not done very well in explaining the trinity so as to maintain the oneness of God. It is time for starting over with fresh words that convey

---

[22] The biblical stories speak to me at a deeper level than all other stories.

relational meaning. We cannot solve old problems by continuing to use the same language that created the problems in the first place. Perhaps, the church, like a crustacean, needs to shed its theological skin every few years, so that it may grow a new one.

I believe one way of starting over with fresh ideas is to make Kindness our new trinity!

I believe God is kind to all living things.

I believe Jesus is kind and calls us to be kind to others.

I believe Spirit is Jesus alive in the church teaching kindness.

As an archetypical image, kindness has transforming energy that heals and reconciles. With an invitation to join in ecumenical dialogue for writing a new trinitarian statement of faith, I end this introductory chapter with the prayer that closes our Bible: "I pray that Jesus will be kind to all of you."[23]

My faith response is: I cannot give all the kindness the world needs, but the world needs all the kindness I can give.

---

[23] Revelation 22:21, CEV.

CHAPTER ONE

God as Relational Kindness

God, you brought me safely through birth, and you protected me as a baby at my mother's breast. From the day I was born I have been in your tender care, and from my birth you have been by my side.[24]

God's "tenderness is directed towards each actual occasion, as it arises."[25]

All theistic religions, those affirming faith in God, have attempted to understand the nature of God and how God relates to the people of God and the world. In one sense God is beyond all human thoughts and wrapped in mystery. The biblical writers recognized this. Isaiah wrote that God's thoughts are not our thoughts and our ways are not God's ways.[26] Expressing his thoughts about God, Paul said, "We see in a mirror dimly" [27] and "We speak God's wisdom in a mystery."[28]

---

[24]Author's paraphrase of Psalm 22:9-10.

[25] Alfred North Whitehead. *Process and Reality*. Corrected Edition, Edited.by David Ray Griffin and Donald W. Sherburne. New York: The Free Press, 1978, p. 105.

[26] Isaiah 55:8-9.

[27] 1 Corinthians 13:12.

[28] 1 Corinthians 2:7.

From the Bible, we know God revealed in the prophets and in Jesus as a uniquely personal and relational God, best described for me as creative responsive kindness. Jesus' gentle teachings especially capture this central truth about God: God is kind. As the creative impulse and adventurous energy that gives value to all of life, God is mystery. Yet God is present in the coming into being of all things. God calls all things into existence and tenderly guides and nurtures all things through the ages. The Psalmist especially saw his life in these relational terms: God, you brought me safely through birth, and you protected me as a baby at my mother's breast. From the day I was born I have been in your tender care, and from my birth you have been by my side.[29]

The Psalms are best seen as joyful songs that were grounded in the goodness of God. Psalm 5 is a good example: "Let all who run to you for protection always sing joyful songs. Provide shelter for those who truly love you and let them rejoice. Our Lord, you bless those who live right, and you shield them with your kindness."[30]

Psalm 4 is an evening prayer for kindness: "There are some who ask, 'Who will be good to us?' Let your kindness, Lord, shine brightly on us. You brought me more happiness than

---

[29]Author's paraphrase of Psalm 22:9-10.

[30] Psalm 5:11-12, CEV.

a rich harvest of grain and grapes. I can lie down and sleep soundly because you, Lord, will keep me safe." [31]

Perhaps the greatest Psalm of loving kindness is Psalm 23. This Good Shepherd Psalm ends with these tender words: "Your kindness and love will always be with me each day of my life, and I will live forever in your house, Lord." [32] The Hebrew word, chesed, is found dozens of times throughout the rest of the Psalms and is often translated as loving kindness.

This image of God's kindness that Israel sang of often is also found in the Old Testament prophets like Isaiah and Hosea. Isaiah's prayer is "Please, Lord, be kind to us! We depend on you. Make us strong each morning, and come to save us when we are in trouble."[33] Here is Isaiah's answer to how God heard his prayer for kindness: Our God has said, encourage my people! Give them comfort. Speak kindly to Jerusalem and announce good news: Clear a path in the desert! Make a straight road for the Lord, our God is here! Just as shepherds care for their flocks, God will carry you in arms of compassion and gently lead you.[34]

Hosea speaks with the same tender image of God: When Israel was a child, I loved him, and I called my son out of Egypt. I took Israel by the arm and taught them to walk. I

---

[31] Psalm 4:6-8, CEV.

[32] Psalm 23:6, CEV.

[33] Isaiah 33:2, CEV.

[34] See Isaiah 40:1-11, CEV.

led them with kindness and with love, not with ropes. I held them close to me. Like a mother I bent down to feed them.[35]

In learning these sacred scriptures of his people, Jesus spiritually shook hands with Isaiah and Hosea. He daily shaped his ministry from the suffering servant songs of Isaiah and the tender story and example of Hosea. In Jesus' gentle teachings and his unique response to God's call, we see God present in the world and acting for the world in kind ways. In the words of Whitehead, God's "tenderness is directed toward each actual occasion, as it arises."[36]

When centered in God's creative loving kindness we live and move and have our being in a circle of kindness that takes in the whole world. God is in us and for us, in the world and for the world. In a sense, love and kindness expressed in the prophets and in Jesus do not define God; God exists before human love and kindness. God revealed in the prophets and in the gentle teachings of Jesus defines these relational terms of love and kindness for us. Jesus was responsive to God's love aims and purposes for his life and became more God conscious with each self-actualization.[37]

---

[35] Hosea 11:1-4, author's paraphrase of CEV. In Hosea we especially see the tension between kindness and vengeance. Hosea 13 is one of the most doom filled and violent chapters in the Bible. Yet this lament chapter, like many Psalms, is preceded by the gentleness of chapter 11 and followed by chapter 14 with the promise of forgiveness and restoration, producing bountiful fruit. Jesus certainly knew both of these themes, kindness and vengeance. He chose to model kindness.

[36] Whitehead, op. cit., p. 105.

[37] I am using God-consciousness as Friedrich Schleiermacher did in *The Christian Faith* (2 vols.). Harper & Row, Publishers, 1963, p. 94f. I have added to Schleiermacher's use of God consciousness as a way of

Jesus' God consciousness, the very real existence of God in Jesus, enabled him to be more conscious of the needs of others in an ever widening circle of loving kindness, and thus more fully divine and human. Jesus' consciousness of God is unique in that it occurred in "the fullness of time" as the culmination of more than a thousand years of covenantal history in which God nurtured Israel as a mother tenderly nurtures her child.[38]

Jesus spoke to God as a child would speak to a parent, confidently and securely. Jesus saw God like a kind father and nurturing mother.

> The biblical image of faith in the time of Jesus was of a child wrapped in the folds of a mother's garment where there is security, comfort, nurturing, love, kindness, and hope.

Psalm 131 serves as a good summary of Israel's faith modeled by Jesus, "I have learned to feel safe and satisfied,

---

understanding Jesus' divinity Emmanuel Kant's "ideal of moral perfection." (See *Religion within the Limits of Reason Alone*, pp. 54 ff.)

[38] See Hosea 11 for this mother child imagery for envisioning God.

just like a child on its mother's lap. People of God, you must trust God now and forever."[39]

God's loving kindness involves God as present in the world. Responsive love is often suffering love. God suffers with the world. We know from **personal experience** what Isaiah, Hosea, and Jesus learned: that loving kindness is a sympathetic response from one person to another. True kindness feels what the other person is feeling, rejoicing in their joys and hurting with their pains. We would doubt that a husband loves his wife if he were not aware of her feelings and if his feelings did not reflect her feelings and respond with kindness.

As we experience God revealed in the prophets and in Jesus, we find God rejoicing with us in our times of joy and weeping with us in our times of sorrow. Our kindness toward others is based on this responsive kindness we see in God. Our theology should reflect the awe and wonder of God being in the world, in us, and for us, holding us close as a mother wraps her child in the folds of her garments or tenderly holds her child in her lap.

The world does not exist apart from God. God the Gardener loves natural beauty. The Gardener, in tenderness, hovers over every blade of grass and whispers, "Awake. Grow. Grow beautiful and green." Meadows grow, giving way to gurgling streams, water plants, butterflies, hummingbirds, flitting from red, orange, and yellow

---

[39] Father's also provide security, nurture, comfort, love, kindness, and hope. I am seeking a balance.

flowers. Beautiful gardens answer the call and over eons of time, all nature is lured toward ever enriching possibilities until conditions are right for life forms to emerge. Over billions of years God called forth a world able to support human beings.[40]

Humans are a new song that nature hums, the music swells with each new stanza, giving purpose and meaning. Humans moved from being gatherers in the garden to being gardeners, ever singing nature's love songs. Love, kind acts, and doing the right thing---these are all products of the garden within us that we nurture with God's guidance. Sometimes God's kindness can come through the facial expression of our grandson and granddaughter, or the touch of a friend when we are hurting. In these special moments the music becomes a joint love song that we sing to God moving us to trust God's guidance and listen to that symphony of voices within that guide us to be kind to one another.

God calls and lures the world forward in tenderness, inspiring novel love aims and goals within all parts of creation. God is supremely socially related with the purpose of sharing goodness and loving kindness with all of creation. God, all nature, and humans are interconnected. As God is immanent in the world, I am in nature and nature is in me. As I write these words I am looking at the snow-capped Chugach Mountains of Alaska. I am in the mountains and

---

[40] God's nurturing of all things to this point gives me hope that it will all end well. See my book, *A Center that Holds: Adventures in Kindness* and the chapter on Hope for a fuller development of this theme of eschatology.

the mountains are in me, singing their song, filling every part of my body and spirit with a wealth of beauty. Observing God's beautiful world is a centering experience of tenderness.

The individual as a deciding entity who sings the love songs of nature is not lost in this adventurous process of kindness for all of life is socially related. The God we meet in the beauty of nature and on the pages of the Bible, especially in the tender teachings and actions of Jesus, is in us and for us. The goodness and beauty of the natural world reflects the goodness, grace, beauty, and kindness of God. God is tenderly present in all things. This is not pantheism saying that all things are God. Rather, it is pan-en-theism, saying that God is in all things as "the poet of the world, with tender patience leading"[41] in responsive love.

The call of God toward kindness nurtured in a long covenant of love between God and Israel and supremely revealed in Jesus' tender teachings is a call to all people. In freedom some respond while others deny the call. The Bible is a record of human response to God's gentle call; it tells both the rejection and response to accept and move forward in a creative kindness with God. Some men and women responded in tender and marvelous ways in the Old Testament and New Testament times, as people have in all cultures. For Christians, Jesus is the supreme example of loving kindness. To affirm this does not lessen the role of Moses for Judaism, Mohammed for Islam or Buddha for

---

[41] Whitehead, op. cit. p. 346.

Buddhism, and other important religious teachers. Buddha said often, "My religion is kindness." When any one relates to the God of creative possibilities, creative transformation occurs, bringing harmony and peace. **Gathering around gentle teachings that are present in all religions offers a pathway to peace in our global pluralistic age.**[42]

God's loving kindness is persuasive and luring, not coercive and demanding. Relational love does not seek to control with coercion. Relational power is greatest in its ability to influence others. If we love someone we do not seek to control or pressure them with promises and threats. Instead we try to persuade them with tender luring love to actualize the possibilities for goodness, beauty, and kindness. The gentle Galilean glories of Jesus define power in terms of loving kindness. This is also a good theology for parenting.

Does this emphasis on God's tender persuasive power rather than coercive power make God weak? Does this question have merit? Are humans more at home with coercive power than luring and persuasive power? My parents were gentle and kind, but they were not weak. To manage a family with thirteen children required a tough tenderness, and that is how I would describe God's power.

People who want to have coercive power for themselves and for God often ask, "If God is All-powerful, why doesn't

---

[42] See Todd Outcalt, *The Other Jesus: Stories from World Religions* for many touch points between Judaism, Christianity, Islam, Buddhism, especially in reference to stories about the teachings and actions of Jesus. Kindness is perhaps the most important touch point.

God change things?" One businessman expressed the feeling like this: "If I were God, I would show people who is boss." This man could very well have been the father of a little boy in the cartoons, down on his knees by the bedside, saying his prayers, and almost out of patience with God: "Aunt Stella isn't married yet. Uncle Hubert hasn't got a job. Daddy's hair is still falling out. I'm tired of saying prayers for this family without getting results." We all know of the silence of the sky. The Book of Job turns on it. If God is Almighty as the Apostle's Creed says, why doesn't God rid the world of all its evil? The classic expression of this dilemma is this: If God is all loving, God would want to rid the world of all evil. And if God is all powerful, then God could rid the world of all evil. Since there is a very real presence of evil in the world, God must not be all loving and all powerful. As Christians we affirm that God is all loving. Thus, we need to redefine power, emphasizing not the quantity of power, but the quality of power.

The basic issue is the nature of divine power. The phrase in the Creed, "I believe in God the Father Almighty," invites us to see a different kind of power, a power qualified by a parent's love, a persuasive and luring power that sets novel aims and gently lures us toward fulfilling those aims. This parental image of God, while often overlooked, is a common view of the Bible and is seen most clearly in the gentle teachings of Jesus in the Gospels.

Is this gentle relational love weak? Or is gentle love the one force that slowly but surely transforms our lives, our communities, and our world? God's kindness expressed in Trinitarian relationships and bound up in community relationships of faith, hope, love, joy, and peace may be the most powerful force in the world!

God's power expressed as a power-field of love energies issuing in kindness is transformational. These love energies are seen and experienced in God who relates to us in mysterious ways. This relational God calls all persons into this power field of love energies that transform persons and God's own self. God is first and foremost transformed by the experience of Jesus' tender life, suffering, death, and resurrection. Through Jesus' deep socially developed God-consciousness, God is revealed to us in new and transforming ways of kindness. This is God's own self-revelation. In these special relationships, God wills to be in us and for us, in the world and for the world.

In the closing chapters of *Process and Reality*, Whitehead sought to show how God relates to the world and how the world relates to God. In this major work among his philosophical writings, Whitehead was primarily concerned with elucidating the "primordial" nature of God. This aspect of God gathered all the wealth of potentiality or divine ordering of all possibilities for the world. These possibilities were further defined as God's love aims and purposes for creation. For Whitehead order was not sufficient for explaining the novelty and freshness of the new and keeping the massiveness of the order from degenerating into mere repetition. "It belongs to the goodness of the world that its settled order should deal tenderly with the faint discordant light of the dawn of another age."[43]

The satisfaction of these aims and purposes in tenderness that nothing be lost required Whitehead to present what he described as the "consequent" nature of God, i.e., God's prehension or feeling of all entities in the world. As primordial, God is unchanging in goodness, kindness, and love. As consequent, God is in the world and in us, feeling our sorrow and our joy, our hatred and our love. As we feel God's joy, love, and kindness we are changed; and as God feels our joy, love, and kindness God is changed, for this is the nature of reciprocal loving kindness. Kindness flows from the one to the many, and the many become one in the unity of the harmony of God.

My use of the metaphor, kindness as a Trinitarian term is also useful for combining both the primordial and consequent aspects of God as spelled out by Whitehead. The primordial nature of God is the ground for kindness as this quote from Process and Reality clearly shows: God's "tenderness is directed toward each actual occasion, as it arises."[44] Kindness does not float into the world or into our experience from nowhere. For Whitehead everything is positively somewhere in actuality and in potency everywhere. Thus, using insights from Whitehead, we can interpret kindness as the aim or goal for all of creation. And the consequent nature of God further grounds kindness as

---

[43] *Process and Reality*, p. 339.

[44] Ibid, p. 105.

a tender care that nothing be lost. Every entity is felt by God as an actual entity. As these two roles are relational concepts, they have served as guidelines for elucidating the trinity, a doctrine that seeks to show how God relates to the people of God, first in the Scriptures and also to us. For me, kindness expresses this relationship best.

Kindness as used in the Old Testament carries well the primordial aspect of God. Kindness is a key metaphor for the way the Jewish people experienced God's aims and purposes. Exodus 33:19 defines God as kindness in this foundational "I am" saying. "I am God, and I show mercy and kindness to anyone I choose" (CEV). This verse names Kindness as an ontological aspect of God. So what the Christian belief in the Trinity names as God the Father is best conceived as "God is kind." Kindness is a gender neutral term and communicates well what is meant by the name, Father. The faith of Israel can be stated in these three words: God is kind. The Psalms of Israel are filled with the "loving kindness" of God, and kindness can be seen as the one unfailing response of God. The first part of the trinity can be stated as "I believe God is kind to all living things."

Kindness is also an appropriate metaphor for expressing what is intended in the second part of the Christian trinity: the Son. The next chapter will show how Jesus responded to God's call and self-actualized in his own gentle ministry the love aims and purposes of God wrapped in kindness, becoming the model for all humanity and making it possible for God to be with us and in us in new transforming ways of kindness.

35

CHAPTER TWO

Jesus Actualized God's Kindness

God's love and kindness will shine upon us like the sun that rises in the sky. On us who live in the dark shadow of death, this light will shine to guide us into a life of peace.[45]

When one tugs at a single kind love word of Jesus, one finds it is attached to the heart of God.[46]

The kindness of Jesus, the bright morning star, shines throughout the New Testament, especially the Gospels of Matthew, Mark, Luke, and John. As presented in these Gospels, the kindness of Jesus reveals God's love and kindness and has transforming energy. The kindness we show to ourselves, our family, and to all living things is the greatest healing and hopeful force in the world.

The kindness of Jesus is an historical fact that is undeniable. The trend today is to deny that one can write a biography of Jesus. Albert Schweitzer's book, *The Quest of the Historical Jesus*, has been seen as the death knell to this search. My own search for the historical Jesus started in 1964 in seminary and has continued for the past fifty years. In a graduate seminar on "The Search for the Historical Jesus" we read

---

[45] Luke 1:78-79. Compare Isaiah 9:2.

[46] Dwayne Cole

biographies of Jesus written in English, French, and German. Since my graduate studies I have tried to keep up with the search for the historical Jesus through Rudolf Bultmann, the post-Bultmannians, and the Jesus seminars. This search has given and continues to give us valuable insight into the life and teachings of Jesus.

My hermeneutic, my biblical principle of interpretation is simply this: Jesus' kindness transforms suffering, changing our lives and our world. The abiding and eternal significance of this principle is independent of historical knowledge of Jesus, i.e., the ability to write a biography of Jesus. My writings on the gentle teachings of Jesus, for which this book on the trinity dovetails nicely, demonstrate that one can write an historical account of the teachings of Jesus. The kindness of Jesus is an undeniable historical fact; and that Jesus' tender teachings and actions as the actualization of God's kindness has transforming healing power is also an historical fact well documented in personal experience.

The abiding and eternal significance of kindness as a hermeneutic for interpreting the life and teachings of Jesus is independent of historical knowledge. To use Carl Jung's thought: kindness is an archetype layered in the collective unconsciousness of most cultures. Kindness may even be isolated as an evolutionary principle. The survival of the fittest often meant being kind to insiders and creating community to offer security for growth and development. That Jesus' personal consciousness focused heavily on kindness is undeniable. Jesus self-actualized the kindness of God that he found expressed beautifully in the Psalms and prophets of his sacred Scriptures. Yet, what so often happens is that in writing our personal biographies of Jesus we skip over Jesus' kindness and paint Jesus from our own personal consciousness and personal interest. This is what I have learned from my fifty year search for the historical Jesus.

> Each time we try to paint Jesus in our image he breaks free; and comes to us as one unknown, as he did to his disciples by the Sea of Galilee long ago. Those who receive Jesus with fresh eyes learn in their own experience illumined by the Spirit of the risen Jesus who he is; and in following their lives are transformed by kindness.

I am more confident than many current biblical scholars that one can find the historical Jesus in the Gospels of the New Testament. The critical question for this book on the trinity is to what extent the kindness of Jesus is empowered by God's Spirit and united as one with God.

The miracle of the Gospels is that in and through the inspired words of the four Gospel writers, Jesus' words continue to live and speak. Gospel writing may be called an anamnesis form of writing. Anamnesis comes from the transliteration of a Greek word meaning "remembering." As acts of remembering, the gospels are not strictly speaking historical biographies about Jesus. However, this could be said for all biographical writing, for all are interpreted remembrance and not "pure" facts. There is no un-interpreted and un-biased remembering and putting remembering into written words. To be a faithful witness does not simply mean passing on tradition. The New Testament evangelists in announcing good news were responsible for letting the good news meet the changing needs of their present communities. The vital needs of the early Christian movement changed quickly and drastically following the crucifixion of Jesus.

In the anamnesis form of writing, the faithful telling of the past stories of Jesus are united with the faithful proclamation in the present worshipping communities of the evangelists. The time interval is bridged and Spirit inspired words of Jesus are experienced. What links the past and present creating a new future is the experienced presence of God in each new act of kindness; and these are trinitarian concerns.

The same symbiotic action can be seen in the life and teachings of Jesus. The consciousness of God's presence linked the human Jesus with Israel's prophets and psalmist, his religious past. The linking of past and present creates a new unity in Jesus' teachings, and those who hear Jesus hear the word of God. The sacred past is remembered and re-enacted in Jesus' teachings. As Jesus' mode of vision renders the past as present, when the followers of Jesus remember his tender words and actions they are linked with the historical Jesus. In remembering all are drawn into the "we circle." The core of the "we circle" are the eyewitnesses who saw and heard Jesus speak. In remembering we are linked with the "we circle" and thereby linked with the historical Jesus who becomes present to us today. Remembering overcomes the time interval. As Jesus is remembered he becomes a once for all time event. In the Church's liturgy the generations are united as one as we become one with "the great cloud of witnesses."

The act of remembering and the "we circle" formula are supported by the role of the Paraclete or Spirit in the New Testament. The Spirit of God infuses and inspires the church's proclamation and the words of Jesus continue to speak, become more deeply understood, and grasped in faith. In the faithful linking of past and present, the historical Jesus steps out of the New Testament stories as they are proclaimed and into our lives as the living word of God! And this is the trinity.

In order to fully understand how truly kind Jesus was and see his kindness as the actualization of God's kindness, we must briefly capsule the period and environment of Jesus' life. All of life is socially related and we are shaped by the social circumstances of our life and our historical epoch.

This is the meaning of the phrase in the New Testament that says, "Jesus was born in the fullness of time."[47]

The Jewish nation in Jesus' time was a small weak nation in a remote and infertile land with only a few exceptions. Since the return from the Babylonian exile, 586-538 B.C.E, the Jewish people had very little political independence. They were dominated by a long succession of foreign powers from the Persians to the Romans. Yet Israel's faith in God was like a vital nerve center that sustained her in these perilous times.

Jesus' Cultural and Social Environment

The Pharisees, seeking to sustain and strengthen faith, first appeared under the rule of John Hyrcanus (135-105 B.C.E). The name "Pharisee" is generally interpreted as "the separate ones." They had the reputation of excelling the rest of the nation in the observance of the law. This group gave birth to many of the oral laws and traditions that governed the daily life of the average Jew in Jesus' time. Jesus had to justify his gentle words and actions to the Pharisees.[48]

The Sadducees held what little political authority the Jews possessed. The Sadducean high priests were the connecting link with the foreign powers. They were a small group,

---

[47] See Galatians 4:4.

[48] For an excellent book on the Jewish sects in the time of Jesus see Joachim Jeremias, *Jerusalem in the Time of Jesus*. This makes it all the more significant that Jesus answered God's call of kindness and conducted a ministry characterized by tenderness.

more political than religious, and exercised a widespread influence. They were even harsher than the Pharisees in their dealings with Jesus.

A third major Jewish sect, the Essenes, outdid the Pharisees in piety by withdrawing into small communities where they lived simple and abstentious lives. The wilderness west of the Dead Sea was a favorite location for their communities. The Dead Sea Scrolls discovered in the middle of the twentieth century have shed light on the Essenes and shown possible connections with John the Baptist and thereby Jesus. This connection is minor and could be explained by the syncretistic nature of Jewish life in the first century rather than a direct link.

The party of the Zealots made up a fourth group among the Jews. It was founded by Judas the Galilean who stirred up a rebellion against the Romans in 6 C.E.[49] The Zealots were opposed to paying tribute to pagan emperors, for God was the only true King. They usually concealed daggers and were ready to destroy the hated Romans when the opportunity was presented to them. At least one of Jesus' disciples was a Zealot.

There have been periodic attempts to tag Jesus with the "zealot" name, most recently Reza Aslan.[50] Aslan's central thesis seems to be that since Jesus grew up in Galilee where

---

[49] Acts 5:37.

[50] Reza Aslan, *Zealot: The Life and Times of Jesus of Nazareth.*

the zealot spirit was rampant, he was shaped by this spirit.[51] Aslan places a lot of weight on the one passage in Luke 22:35-38 where Jesus asked his disciples as tensions increased with the ruling authorities to sell some of their clothes and buy a sword if they did not have one. When the disciples said that they already had two swords, Jesus replied, "It is enough." This could be translated, "It is enough about that!" It was common advice to take a sword on dangerous trips in the time of Jesus. This advice is found only in Luke 22:37; and Luke places it in the context of a quote from Isaiah 53:12, a suffering servant song. The spirit of the suffering servant who willingly gives life would certainly give a new slant to this advice of buying a sword.

Jesus' response after the remark about already having two swords would seem to support this interpretation. In frustration about the disciples not understanding his role, Jesus says, in effect, "that is enough about swords." The one clear principle from Jesus' life and teachings is that one has the right to give life but never to take life.[52] History shows many examples of men and women who rose above the spirit of their times and became shapers of events not

---

[51] No doubt this is partly true. A thesis of this chapter is that one is shaped by one's epoch and this partly accounts for the diversity of the Bible written over a thousand year period. However there are individuals who are able to rise above the spirit of their times, and Jesus was one of these persons.

[52] To be sure Jesus struggled with all of these human responses to God and to others. His own disciples according to John 6 tried to force him to become their king. Jesus's temptations can be seen as a time when Jesus struggled with the nature of his life and teachings. What kind of leader and teacher would he be? Jesus came down of the side of a suffering servant like Second Isaiah and the gentle example of Hosea.

followers---Abraham Lincoln, Gandhi, Martin Luther King, Jr., and Mother Teresa to name a few.

The Herodians are mentioned in the New Testament as enemies of Jesus, both in Galilee[53] and in Jerusalem.[54] The term apparently denotes an attitude rather than a political party or religious sect. It seems to refer to the Jews who supported the Herodian rule and the Romans.

The vast majority of Palestinian Jews were unaffiliated with any of these groups. These multitudes were known as people of the land, "Am-haaretz." The Pharisees felt that these common people from the country were ignorant of or indifferent to the Mosaic Law; thus, they were considered immoral and irreligious.

Without excluding the others, it was more self-exclusion, it was basically this group of common people who were recipients of Jesus' gentle, Galilean teachings. Though the Pharisees saw them as worthless outcasts, Jesus saw them with compassion because they were helpless like "sheep without a shepherd."[55] Jesus chose to become like the Good Shepherd of Psalm 23 and Ezekiel 34, tenderly caring for the poor and needy. In choosing this path, Jesus perfectly incarnated the kindness of God expressed in Israel's best

---

[53] Mark 3:6.

[54] Matthew 22:16; Mark 12:13.

[55] Matthew 9:36.

faith and practice. In choosing kindness, Jesus consciously rejected the path of the zealots, the path of vengeance.

Jesus' Birth and Early Years

The simplicity and gentleness of the birth narratives of Jesus and his tender teachings are all the more striking against the Jewish cultural and social background given above. The nativity scene evokes the best feelings in our human nature: the devout mother and father, the child in a bare manger, the shepherds and wise men who come to worship him, and the angels who bridge the lowly earthly scene with the heavenly spheres, a bridging which the life, death, and resurrection of Jesus would make complete.

It is almost unbelievable! The human Jesus was born in a remote nation in the humblest of circumstances and was cradled in a manger, perhaps a feed trough.[56] Yet, in these humble circumstances, the baby Jesus was surrounded by gentle Mary and Joseph, simple shepherds, and glorious angelic choruses. The Gospel writers, writing 70-90 years after the birth of Jesus, were able to see from the gentle teachings of Jesus how God and Jesus had become one in kindness; and see how Jesus' faithful response to God's call enabled God to come near to people. In Luke's words, God came in tenderness and the bright light of heaven shone upon all who walked in darkness.[57] Whitehead interpreted this as God meeting each rising occasion with tenderness.

---

[56] It is important to see that the birth of Jesus did not violate our understanding of human nature.

[57] Luke 1:78.

Jesus responded to the call of God and revealed God's kindness in his tender teachings.

Luke's Gospel is the only one which has anything to say about Jesus' early years. After the shepherds' visit, the story continues with the circumcision of the child on the eighth day of his life, in fulfillment of the law the child was formally given the Greek name Jesus which is the same as Joshua in Hebrew.[58] It was a common name meaning "he saves" or in its full form, "Jehovah saves." The presentation of Jesus in the Temple places us once again in the very heart of Jewish piety and worship. In keeping with the Mosaic Law, Mary observed the purification rites by presenting an offering of a pair of doves or two young pigeons while at the same time presenting the child to God.[59] The offering indicates that Mary and Joseph were poor. According to Leviticus 12, the offering called for a lamb but mothers who were poor could substitute the less expensive offering.

In the Temple, Joseph and Mary encountered a good, God-fearing man named Simeon who was waiting for Israel to be saved. When Simeon took Jesus in his arms to bless him-- an appropriate symbol for the one who would later take children in his arms and bless them--Simeon burst forth in praise to God: Now Lord, you have kept your promise, and you may let your servant go in peace. With my own eyes I have seen your salvation, which you have prepared in the

---

[58] Luke 2:21; cf. Genesis 17:9-14; Leviticus 12:3.

[59] Leviticus 12:1-4, 6; Luke 2:22-24.

presence of all peoples: a light to reveal your will to the Gentiles and bring glory to your people Israel.[60]

There was also in the Temple an elderly prophetess, a widow named Anna (Hannah in Hebrew). Anna worshipped God day and night, fasting and praying, never leaving the Temple. She too recognized who the baby was and with thanksgiving to God "spoke about the child to all who were waiting for God to set Jerusalem free."[61]

Having completed the requirements of the law, Joseph, Mary, and Jesus returned to their home town of Nazareth in Galilee. In Galilee Jesus grew and became strong, increasing in favor (graciousness) with God and with humans.[62]

These birth and infancy narratives are stamped throughout with the mark of Jewish piety. We meet Judaism at its best as the cradle of Jesus. We see humble, lowly, gentle servants of God who have spent their whole lifetime glorifying God and waiting patiently for God's deliverance and salvation.

These accounts make it clear that God comes to waiting people, taking the initiative and drawing near to them. In kindness God came to lift up the lowly and gentle servants.[63] The heart throb of tenderness and gentleness beats

---

[60] Luke 2:29-32.

[61] Luke 2:36-38.

[62] Luke 2:52.

[63] Titus 3:4; Luke 1:48, 52.

throughout. Not only is God kind and gentle, Joseph is gentle and considerate of Mary. Joseph was a bridge for Jesus' understanding of one who would become a heavenly Father to him.

Also, we have seen that the lowly are exalted or glorified. Heavenly glories shine throughout these narratives and will continue to shine through Jesus' gentle Galilean glories. When reading these Gospel accounts of the birth of Jesus we need to remember that they were written 70-90 years after the birth of Jesus, and while they are historical they have naturally taken on some legendary and mythic qualities.

The only other glimpse of Jesus the Gospels give us of his early years was his visit to the Temple at the age of twelve. On this visit Mary and Joseph miss Jesus and began to look for him. They find him in the Temple asking serious questions and saying, I must be about My Father's business.[64]

This seems to be a very significant time in Jesus' maturation. The kindness, gentleness, and love of God that had been prefigured in Mary and Joseph and his faith community were now affirmed as being rooted in God. While this was a significant insight or rite of passage for Jesus, he went back to Galilee with Joseph and Mary where he continued to grow in body and in wisdom, gaining favor with God and humans. The Greek word translated as "favor" here is a form of χαρις. It is usually translated in the New Testament

---

[64] Luke 2:49. While these stories have taken on legendary tones they still reflect historical events.

as grace. It can also be translated as kindness.[65] It describes the qualities of grace and kindness that make a person attractive or favorable. It also describes the attitude of goodwill, respect, or approval of others toward a gracious and kind person.

Jesus returned home to Galilee. Home for Jesus included four brothers: James, Joses (or Joseph), Judas, and Simon. He also had sisters but we are not told how many nor are we told their names. Clearly Jesus grew up in a large household which was no doubt lively. Having grown up in a family where I was the eighth of thirteen children I can vouch for this.

How much formal education Jesus received is not known. Joseph would have started Jesus' education in the home as the Jewish law commanded. Every pious Jewish father, and we are told that Joseph was devout,[66] taught his son the Shema: Israel, remember this! The Lord--and the Lord alone--is our God. Love the Lord your God with all your heart, with all your soul, and with all your strength. Never forget these commandments that I am giving you today, i.e., center your life on these teachings of love. Teach them to

---

[65] The American Bible Society's *Contemporary English Version* often translates χαρις as kindness. See below for a treatment of χαρις. I have checked the usage of this word from Plato up through the time of Jesus and found that they are justified in translating χαρις as kindness. See my *Book of Revelation: Jesus' Kindness Transforms Suffering*, where I used kindness as my hermeneutic for interpreting John's message to the suffering followers of Jesus in the seven Churches.

[66] Matthew 1:19.

your children.[67] Jesus made this the first commandment of all of his teachings.[68] It is interesting that Jesus added "with all your mind" to his presentation of the great commandment. We know that Jesus had an active and perceptive mind.

In addition to learning from Joseph at home, Jesus probably attended the synagogue school in Nazareth. How much, if any, formal education he had, of course, is not known. A popular view today is to see Jesus as a simple uneducated carpenter. The Gospels themselves point in the other direction. In the Gospel of Mark the verb, "teach" occurs seventeen times, and in all but one of these Jesus is the subject. Jesus is very often called teacher by his disciples and his opponents. The fact that Jesus was called teacher by his opponents would seem to indicate that they recognized his qualification to teach. According to Luke, Jesus read the Scripture lesson in the synagogue at Nazareth.[69] In his teaching he assumed that his hearers had heard their scriptures read and some probably had read some biblical scrolls. He would often ask, "Have you not read…?[70] Jesus had an almost encyclopedic knowledge of his Holy Scriptures and with penetration and independence he combined and interpreted them in a unique way. Jesus read and spoke Aramaic. He knew Hebrew well enough to read it in the synagogue. He, of economic necessity, had a

---

[67] Deuteronomy 6:4-7.

[68] Mark 12:28-30.

[69] Luke 4:16-20.

[70] Mark 2:25, 12:10; Matthew 12:5; 19:4; 21:16, 42.

carpenter's command of common Greek, which was becoming the common language of his day. Jesus' study of the Old Testament Scriptures helped to shape his understanding of his ministry and message. This was especially true of the Suffering Servant passages of Isaiah.

Kindness in Jesus' Teachings

God's love and kindness will shine upon us like the sun that rises in the sky. On us who live in the dark shadow of death, this light will shine to guide us into a life of peace (Luke 1:78-79, CEV).

The goal of the Christian should be to live in harmony with the kind teachings of Jesus.

Serving for almost fifty years as a parish minister, I learned a lot about the need for tenderness in our human relationships. We all fight hard battles and need at least a bushel of kindness a day. Every person and every family needs gentleness to survive.

> Simple acts of kindness to oneself, one's family, and to all living things are the most powerful transformers in the world.

My own father and mother were examples of kindness for me and my six brothers and six sisters. My father often prayed public prayers in our little country Church, and one of his favorite expressions was "Kind Father." He started

51

his prayers with this address and repeated it several times throughout the prayer. He said it so many times that I was embarrassed about it. Of course, it doesn't take much to embarrass an adolescent when it comes to his or her parents.

Today I treasure this memory and it has helped me to be a kinder person. My mother and father taught me by word and example that God is kind. They were gentle and loving parents and they made it easy for all thirteen of us to believe in a gentle and loving God. For their children, parents truly are the first bridge to the love of God, as are all caregivers.

This book springs from this source and holds up the kindness of Jesus as the guiding light for our lives, our Churches, and our world. It is the nature of light to draw us in to its center and reveal newness. The Gospel of Luke expresses this truth well: *God's love and kindness will shine upon us like the sun that rises in the sky. On us who live in the dark shadow of death, this light will shine to guide us into a life of peace.*[71]

In contrast to the bleak gray of much of Palestine, Galilee, especially the plain of Gennesaret, was a very fertile, magnificent garden, inspiring Jesus' bio-philic (love of life) teachings. Jesus preached gentle Galilean glories in this delightful countryside. The flowers of the fields, birds of the air, farmers sowing seed, and fishermen casting their nets all

---

[71] Luke 1:78-79, CEV.

came into Jesus' teachings and parables. This earthly beauty gave Jesus a vision of heavenly glory; and the vision was grounded in earthly realities, shining on the highways and byways of Galilee in Jesus' tenderness and gentleness, transforming lives.

Let me hasten to say that Galilee was not all sweetness and light, neither was the rugged carpenter from Nazareth. Not for a minute do I imply that with this theme of kindness. Personally speaking, I had to learn to balance kindness and toughness in my own life. I grew up as the eighth of thirteen children on a working farm and life was sometimes rough as a cob. I played football for four years of high school, playing both offensive and defensive right end for the whole game. I worked in a wire mill on the "graveyard" shift to help pay my way through college. In that mill I received a real lesson about toughness and heard plenty of "gutter" language that was more suitable for the halls of hell than the halos of heaven. At least this experience prepared me for unruly deacon and elder meetings in the church more than seminary did. Building houses for seven years and going through great success and failure also revealed a tough side of life to me. However, my basic nature still tilts toward tenderness due to my family background and the gentle teachings of Jesus seem to reveal the same about Jesus. As Jesus worked through his own temptations and chose kindness as his guiding principle for interpreting the scriptures and life situations, each of us has to choose our way. I have chosen kindness as my way.

This background makes Jesus' kindness all the more amazing with transforming centering power. Jesus' disciples were slowly transformed by Jesus' gentle teachings and actions. And the kindness of Jesus is a vision of world peace for every age.

Jesus' Gentle and Kind Words

Does the New Testament verify that Jesus was gentle and kind? The Greek New Testament does not have just one term for kindness. Several Greek words are used by different writers to describe gentleness in its various aspects. The same is true of other concepts like love (αγαπη, ερος, φιλια). The Greek terms that best denote the gentle attitude are πραυς and πραυτης.

Πραυς, Πραυτης (gentle, gentleness)

In reference to persons, πραυς and πραυτης, the noun and adjective form, are best translated as gentle and gentleness. The two terms are used about 15 times in the Greek New Testament and may also be translated as kind, meek, humble, friendly, or pleasant, in both adjective and noun forms. As used in these different forms the words imply gentleness as opposed to rough, harsh, or violent. Gentleness is a synonym of ελεος, mercy. It is an active attitude not passive submission.

Among the Greeks, a kind, gentle, and friendly attitude toward family and friends was highly prized. It was the quality of a great soul like Socrates. However, it was alright to be harsh to one's enemies. For Plato πραυς was the mark of the ideal kingdom. For Aristotle it was a mean between anger which had a positive value and indifference.

In its Hebrew form, πραυς is used twelve times in the Old Testament. It is used only once in the Pentateuch, the first five books of the Old Testament, but it is a significant summary description of the great leader, Moses---"Moses was a humble (gentle) man, more humble than anyone else on earth."[72]

In the Old Testament kindness is rooted in God. The inheritance of the land promised to Abraham and his descendants comes to the gentle who wait---"The humble will possess the land and enjoy prosperity and peace."[73]

These eschatological overtones are expressed as a messianic prophecy in Zechariah 9:9, "Rejoice, rejoice, people of Zion! Shout for joy, you people of Jerusalem! Look, your king is coming to you! He comes triumphant and victorious, but gentle and riding on a donkey."

In the New Testament, the mission of Jesus is the fulfillment of gentleness. In fact, it is the self-designation of Jesus in Matthew 11:28-30--"Come to me, all of you who are tired from carrying heavy loads, and I will give your rest. Take my yoke and put it on you, and learn from me, because I am gentle and humble in spirit; and you will find rest. For the yoke I will give you is easy and the load I will put on you is light." In interpreting the New Testament, the titles and descriptions that Jesus applies to himself should carry the greatest weight. Jesus did not hesitate to say, "I am gentle."

---

[72] Numbers 12:3.

[73] Psalm 37:9-11.

In fulfillment of eschatological hope, Jesus said, "Blessed are the gentle, they will receive what God has promised!"[74] As a further fulfillment of prophecy,[75] Jesus entered Jerusalem on what we call Palm Sunday as king---"Now this occurred to fulfill what was spoken by the prophet: 'Tell the daughter of Zion your King is now coming to you, Gentle, and riding on a donkey, Yea, on the colt of a beast of burden.'"[76]

This self-designation of Jesus as gentle is all the more significant when set against the zealot and political messianic expectations of the first century in Galilee. The Gospel of John tells us that after the feeding of the five thousand these feelings were so strong that the crowd came and sought to force Jesus to become their king.[77]

That Jesus was πραυς, tender of heart, is also supported by the Letters of Paul in the New Testament and in non-biblical sources like the Gospel of Thomas, the Sibylline Oracles, and Pistis Sophia. In Second Corinthians chapter ten, verse one, Paul wrote, "Jesus himself was humble and gentle." Colossians 3:12 grounds kindness in the being of God, "You are God's people so be gentle, kind, humble, and meek." Titus 3:4 also describes God as kind.

---

[74] Matthew 5:5.

[75] Zechariah 9:9, quoted above.

[76] Matthew 21:4-5. Williams translation.

[77] John 6:14-15.

ταπεινος, ταπεινοω, ταπεινωσις

This group of Greek words occurs thirty-four times in the New Testament, and they are usually translated "lowly", but they carry the connotation of kindness and gentleness. Here we will be concerned for the one occurrence that refers to Jesus. Again it is significant in that it is a self- designation, like πραυς. Jesus said of himself, "I am gentle (πραυς) and lowly (ταπεινοω) of heart (Matthew 11:29).

χρηστος

Jesus used χρηστος twice, once to describe the nature of God as kind to the ungrateful and wicked[78] and once as a self-designation, describing himself as one who is kind or merciful in what he requires of those who come to him.[79] It is important to see how χρηστος was used in the Septuagint in reference to God. A key passage is found in Exodus 34:6, "I am who I am, and I am kind and patient with my people, I show great love and I can be trusted." Here kindness takes on the quality of good character. God can be trusted to act with loving kindness toward the people of God, and this is the basis of the covenant God forms with the people of God. Even when Israel failed God, God continued to be kind and forgiving. In this context kindness takes on the qualities of patience and forgiveness.

---

[78] Luke 6:35.

[79] Matthew 11:30.

Paul understood kindness in this way as well. In Romans 2:4 he writes about the "fullness of the χρηστητος, kindness, of God and God's patience, μακροθυμιας. In Romans 11:22 Paul speaks of the kindness of God being shown for the ones who have fallen away from God. In these uses of kindness Paul is true to the Old Testament understanding of the gracious action of God and he sees this fulfilled in the actions of Jesus. In Galatians 5:22-23 Paul listed kindness as one of the fruits of the Spirit that should be growing in the life of Christians.

1 Peter 2:2-3, shows the saving action of kindness. "Like new born infants, long for the pure spiritual milk, so that by it you may grow into salvation. If indeed you have tasted that the Lord is good and kind, χρηστος.

The crowning verse on kindness in the New Testament for Christians is Ephesians 4:32---"Be kind and merciful, and forgive others, just as God forgave you because of Christ." This key verse links kindness with forgiveness and anchors these qualities in God's own actions with the gentle ministry of Jesus.

ελεος

Ελεος occurs three times in Matthew and is usually translated as mercy. The Good News Bible translates it as kindness, its original Old Testament meaning. This can be seen in Matthew 9:9-11, which reports Jesus' call of Matthew to discipleship. After Jesus called Matthew, he was having a meal in Matthew's house with other tax collectors and outcasts. Some Pharisees saw this and asked Jesus' disciples, "Why does Jesus eat with such people?" Jesus heard them and answered, "People who are well do not need a doctor, but only those who are sick. Go and find out what is meant by the scripture that says, 'It is kindness that I want, not animal sacrifices.' I have not come to call respectable people, but outcasts." This and the other two passages in Matthew 12:7; 23:23 characterize Jesus' ministry as merciful kindness toward the outcasts and demand the same for the disciples who would follow Jesus.

Ελεος, mercy, occurs six times in Luke. Five of these are in the birth announcements of John and Jesus and refer to the wonderful kindness and tender mercy God is showing toward the people of God.[80] Luke 1:78 is most relevant to the theme of "Gentle Galilean Glories:" "Our God is merciful and tender. God will cause the bright dawn of salvation to rise on us and to shine from heaven on all those who live in the dark shadow of death, to guide our path to peace."

σπλαγχνον, σπλανγχνιζομαι

In Luke 1:78, ελεος is combined with σπλαγχνον and is translated as "tender mercy." The verb form, σπλαγχνιζομαι, occurs twelve times in Matthew, Mark, and Luke, the Synoptic Gospels, and is usually translated as "having compassion." Ten of these represent Jesus as one in whom divine compassion is present. Jesus is moved with

---

[80] Luke 1:50, 54, 58, 72, 78.

compassion toward a man with a dreaded skin disease,[81] the crowd of people who were like sheep without a shepherd,[82] and the hungry crowd.[83]

Jesus also had compassion on the widow of Nain and raised her dead son back to life[84], and with compassion he restored sight to two blind men.[85] The verb, having compassion, also had a central place in three of Jesus' most significant parables: the unforgiving servant who had been forgiven with compassion,[86] the good Samaritan whose heart was filled with compassion when he saw the wounded man lying by the roadside,[87] and the parable of the prodigal son, better called the waiting father, for it is the father who saw the son a long way off and had compassion and ran to meet him.[88]

In all of these teachings of Jesus that use σπλάγχνον and σπλαγχνιζομαι, Jesus' human emotions are described in the strongest terms possible in order to stress the tender compassion with which God claims persons in saving grace.

---

[81] Mark 1:41.

[82] Mark 6:34; Matthew 14:14.

[83] Mark 8:2; Matthew 15:32.

[84] Luke 7:11-17.

[85] Matthew 20:29-34.

[86] Matthew 18:21-35, See verse 34.

[87] Luke 10:25-37, see v. 33. The whole act of the Samaritan was summarized as an act of kindness, see v. 37.

[88] Luke 15:11-32, see v. 20.

This was also true of all the other Greek words we have studied.

χαϱις

The χαϱις word group appears about 175 times in the New Testament, with the majority occurring in the Epistles of Paul. Most English versions of the Bible translate χαϱις as grace or gracious. However, the *Contemporary English Version* of the American Bible Society almost always translates χαϱις as kindness. A survey of the history of the term from its early Greek origins to the time of the New Testament justifies this use of kindness. In both the Old Testament and the New Testament the Hebrew and Greek words usually translated as grace imply a kind turning of one person to another in an act of assistance. God's covenant grace also implies kindness.

Perhaps the most significant uses of χαϱις come in the Book of Revelation. At a time when the followers of Jesus are being persecuted and dying for their faith, John the writer of Revelation holds up a vision of the kind Jesus. The book starts with this prayer: "I pray that you will be blessed with kindness and peace from God, who is and was and is coming. May you receive kindness and peace from Jesus, the faithful witness."[89] Revelation ends with this prayer: "I pray that Jesus will come soon and be kind to all of you."[90]

Yes, Jesus was gentle, lowly, and kind. The word clusters we have examined leave no room for doubt. What struck me was how Jesus described himself as being gentle. Thus, we are on solid ground when we speak of Jesus as kindness. The kindness of God shines in the words and deeds of Jesus. The disciples and the crowds who followed Jesus saw the glory of God shining through his gentle Galilean glories. Can there be any doubt that Jesus lived and taught kindness?

Summary Remarks about the Importance of Kindness

It is my conviction that kindness rings true in all cultures and can be a unifying and centering theme for dialogue in this global pluralistic age between most religions of the world, offering a path to peace. Following the amazing discoveries of the genome project, the mapping of the human chromosomes, biologists speak of the genetic unity of all living things, believing that all organisms descended from the same ancestral life forms. Thus far the genome project has shown that the common ancestor of all living things was similar to single-celled microbes with the simplest molecular composition that goes back several

---

[89] Based on Revelation 1:4-5 from the Greek New Testament.

[90] Based on Revelation 22:20-21, from the Greek New Testament. For a fuller treatment of this use of χαρις as kindness in Revelation see my book, *The Book of Revelation: Jesus' Kindness Transforms Suffering.*

billion years. Thus all life shares a molecular history and is interrelated, interconnected.

This unifying dialogue must take place if we are to have reconciliation between the world religions and find a route to peace. The greatest challenge to theistic religions is the pervasive reality of evil and the misery it leaves in its wake. This unifying and centering theme of kindness is one possible solution to this problem, especially the growing divide between Christianity and Islam.

"Loving kindness" is a major theme in Judaism. The Psalms of the Old Testament are full of this concept that is key to understanding God and God's people. Since Judaism gave birth to Christianity and Islam, the two largest religions in the world, this unifying theme is something all three religions hold in common. "Metta" is a strong concept in Buddhism and carries the meaning of loving kindness or unconditional love. Buddha often spoke of loving kindness as everything. Loving kindness is taught without attachment. In much Buddhist thought love when practiced moves from self to friend, to enemy, and to all beings everywhere. "Karuna" or compassion that leads one to assist others is also key. Meaningful dialogue could be held around the theme of gentle teachings that could transform the relationships between these major religions.

Also, the longer I have lived with the New Testament the more I have become convinced that a major thrust of these sacred scriptures is to show the humanity of Jesus. This makes Jesus' sacrificial death on the cross more meaningful with more transforming power. This approach also opens the door to see that other major religious leaders like Moses, Confucius, Mohammed, Buddha, Gandhi, and Martin Luther King, Jr. can also self-actualize creative love aims and purposes that transform lives and our world.

One may not be able to write a biographical account of the life of Jesus. As seen above, I do believe you can locate in the Gospels the authentic teachings of Jesus, like the gentle teachings. Whether they all come from Jesus or some of them are born as a product of the Gospel writers or the early church community, really do not matter in one sense. They are inspired by Jesus gentle ministry and remain insightful, challenging teachings than can change and transform lives and offer a path to peace.

Jesus' Galilean vision of kindness has flickered through many cultures since the time of Jesus, but it has never been fully realized. Yet it still holds the promise of creative advance, a center that holds, and world transformation.

Meditative Exercise

This chapter on Jesus' kindness holds before us a vision of kindness as transforming energy that slowly but surely changes our lives and our world. Have you experienced kindness in this healing way? Saint Francis is a good example of how life is changed by kindness. You might want to read about his life and influence. Pope Francis is a good model of Jesus' kindness today. Spend at least a few minutes each day praying that you can also model Jesus' kindness. On December 28, 2014, CBS had a special feature on "60 Minutes" about "Inside the Vatican," featuring Pope Francis. The spirit of kindness expresses best what is seen in this Pope. Scott Pelley also had a brief interview with President Barack Obama in which he asked about his encounter with the Pope. Our President highlighted the spirit of kindness and added that it is the spirit of kindness that best describes the life of Jesus. What is your reaction to this special feature about the Pope and the spirit of kindness? Do you agree with our President's assessment of kindness as the best expression of Jesus' life?

CHAPTER THREE

Spirit Empowers God's Kindness Revealed in Jesus

God as Spirit lured creation out of chaos. God as Spirit filled the lives of the prophets who spoke God's message. God's Spirit was present in the birth of Jesus. The same Spirit descended upon Jesus at his baptism and energized Jesus' gentle ministry. Spirit empowered Jesus' followers in Pentecost activity to continue his tender words and actions after the crucifixion and resurrection of Jesus.

The basic role of Spirit in the New Testament is to be an encourager. By linking Spirit with the continuing ministry of Jesus, the New Testament writers join kindness and encouragement. The Hebrew word for Spirit is ruach; and this Hebrew word can be translated as wind or breath of life. It is the word used in Genesis for God breathing the breath of life into humans. This is the way John in Revelation used Spirit in referring to the two witnesses who proclaimed God's message and became martyrs: "Spirit of life is breathed into them by God" (Revelation 11:11). This use of Spirit as the breath of life would have special significance for Jesus' followers in John's churches who are dying as martyrs.

John in Revelation, as does most of the New Testament, virtually equates Spirit and the risen Jesus, seeing their role as one as in Revelation 19:10, "Everyone who tells about Jesus does it by the power of Spirit." For John the church is the new body in which the risen Jesus lives, meeting each rising occasion with the spirit of kindness. The risen Jesus walks in the churches, sees their strengths and weaknesses, and offers to them the centering path to transformation.[91]

In the churches in Ephesus, Smyrna, Pergamum, Thyatira, Sardis, Philadelphia, and Laodicea the Risen Jesus lives and continues his gentle teachings that bring kindness and peace. Revelation 1:5 is addressed to all the churches and captures this consoling truth: "May kindness and peace be yours from Jesus Christ, the faithful witness" (CEV). The role of Jesus and the role of Spirit are one in this compassionate transforming work.

In the prologue to the Gospel of John, God as creative life giving Word is seen as coming into the world in human form in Jesus to bring heavenly light into a dark world. It is important to see that in the prologue as a whole Jesus as a human person cannot be separated from the divine presence of God. John accomplishes this by presenting Jesus as the incarnation of the logos (word). This linkage allows us to see how the human Jesus is different from God but at the same time one with God as a single entity in creating and redeeming.

---

[91] The Book of Revelation, while it is not often recognized, has more teaching on the trinity than any other book of the Bible. See my development of the theme of kindness as a trinitarian metaphor in *The Book of Revelation: Jesus' Kindness Transforms Suffering.*

While John does not connect logos (word) and Sophia (wisdom) with the gift of Spirit in the prologue he does equate risen Jesus and Spirit later in his Gospel as we will see below. Luke and Paul make the connection between Jesus, wisdom, and Sprit in their writings. Luke says that as Jesus matured he was filled with σοφια (wisdom) and χαρις (kindness, grace).[92] Sophia as the feminine companion of God at creation played an important role in Jewish wisdom literature as can be seen in Proverbs 8. Luke in Acts 6:3 connects σοφιας (wisdom) and πνευματος (spirit) as the traits of a good leader.

In 1 Corinthians 12:7-8, Paul connects spirit and wisdom: "The Spirit has given each of us a special way of serving others. Some of us can speak with wisdom while others can speak with knowledge, but these gifts come from the same Spirit." For Paul the continuing ministry of Jesus is empowered by God's Spirit: "You are no longer ruled by the desires of the flesh, but by God's Spirit, who dwells in you. People who don't have the Spirit of the Risen Jesus in them don't belong to Jesus."[93]

In the Gospel of John this union of Jesus and Spirit is affirmed. In the upper room discourse John reports Jesus as saying, "I won't leave you like orphans. I will come back to you. In a little while the people of the world won't be able to see me, but you will see me. And because I live, you will

---

[92] Luke 2:40, 52.

[93] My translation of Romans 8:9.

live."[94] Here Spirit and risen Jesus are one; Jesus is Spirit. Spirit is given to continue the kind teachings of Jesus about forgiveness: "Then Jesus breathed on them and said, 'Receive the Spirit. If you forgive anyone's sins, they will be forgiven.'"[95]

The Gospel of John has four occurrences of παρακλητος (Paraclete) and 1 John has one. This Greek word is formed by joining παρα (by the side of) and κλητος (called) and is best translated as one who is "called to walk along the side of" Jesus' followers in all ages to offer encouragement by meeting each rising occasion with tenderness.

The Epistle of James equates Spirit and σοφια (wisdom) in 1:5 and 3:17 as does Ephesians 1:17. In each case the feminine form of σοφια carries the connotations of kindness. Ephesians opens with the common epistolary greeting: "I pray that God our Father and our Lord Jesus Christ will be kind to you and will bless you with peace."[96] This prayer for kindness is followed by spiritual blessings seen in Jesus' sacrifice on the cross.[97] Then comes another prayer: "I ask the glorious Father and God of our Lord Jesus Christ to give you his Spirit. The Spirit will make you wise (Sophia) and let you understand what it means to know

---

[94] John 14:18-19.

[95] John 20:22-23.

[96] Ephesians 1:2. CEV.

[97] Ephesians 1:3-14.

God."[98] The message of these verses is that God is kind, Jesus is kind, and Spirit is kind.

In 1 John 2:1, Paraclete is linked with Jesus. In the verses that follow 2:1, the role of Spirit is to enable the followers of Jesus to obey his commandments of love and kindness. Clearly the role of Spirit is to continue the kindness of God's presence in the tender teachings of Jesus.

The Epistle of 1 Peter linked God and Spirit with kindness and with Jesus' suffering on the cross. This Epistle actually used the name, Christ, instead of Jesus, but by linking it with the historical suffering of the cross we are justified in saying that Spirit is equated with kindness and with Jesus. We can see this linkage most clearly in the CEV: "Some prophets told how kind God would be to you, and they searched hard to find out more about the way you would be saved. The Spirit of Christ (Jesus) was in them and was telling them how Christ (Jesus) would suffer and then would be given great honor."[99]

All the New Testament writers explored above could write of the risen Jesus and Spirit in the same sentence and make them interchangeable.[100] When discussing God, Jesus, and Spirit we are talking about mystery filled relationships. Let me try to make it as clear as possible. The name, Spirit, is best equated with God's presence in the risen Jesus. The

---

[98] Ephesians 1:17. CEV.

[99] 1 Peter 1:10-11.

[100] Romans 8:9-11.

role of Spirit/Risen Jesus is to continue the gentle, kind, love teachings of the historical Jesus in his new body, the church.

Thus, in summary we can say, using the simplest of terms, God is kind, Jesus is kind, and Spirit is kind.

In this chapter I have used "Spirit" as the name for the continuing reality of Jesus in the church, and I have equated the Risen Jesus and Spirit. This interpretation was shown to be true to the New Testament and will now become the basis for a new approach for understanding the Trinity, a word coined by theologians to explain the ways God relates to us. The word, Trinity, has caused considerable confusion and has not served the church very well. We need a new approach, and we cannot solve the problems of the past by continuing to use the same language that caused the problems in the first place. The next chapter will present one solution to this problem.

We have seen that God is kind, Jesus is kind, and Spirit is kind. Seeing the biblical message in this way is intended to help us think through the way kindness affects us. You might want to spend some prayerful meditation time now focusing on these relational ways of seeing God. Be open to letting Jesus' kind Spirit renew your spirit. Think of specific areas of your life in which you need encouragement and new strength. Read, or if you are musically inclined, sing the hymn, "Breathe on Me, Breath of God."

The following is a kindness creed I wrote. Using it as an example, consider writing your own.

Kindness: The Good News Creed

I believe God is present with us as creative responsive kindness, daily providing transforming love aims and purposes. **God is kind** and meets each and every occasion of our life with kindness.

I believe Jesus self-actualized God's creative tenderness and shared that transforming kindness in his gentle ministry with all persons. The cross of Jesus is the greatest expression of sacrificial love. As a worthy model of all humanity, God raised Jesus to new life; and the resurrection becomes the victory of love over death. **Jesus is kind** and teaches us to be kind to others.

I believe Spirit continues the kindness of Jesus by enabling his followers to remember and understand the gentle teachings of Jesus and extend them into the world with transforming power. **Spirit is kind**.

I believe the Church is the new body of Jesus founded upon the gentle teachings of Jesus, culminating in his sacrificial death and resurrection. The goal and purpose of the church is to maintain, preserve, and extend these gentle teachings, with their power to transform lives, into the world.

CHAPTER FOUR

A Relational Trinity of Kindness

"Do not follow where the path may lead. Go, instead, where there is no path and leave a trail."[101]

One purpose of this book has been to present Jesus' gentle and kind teachings and actions as a new pathway for understanding the trinity. Focusing on these trinitarian truths gives us a center that holds our lives in secure faith, hope, love, joy, and peace.[102] The first three chapters of this book have explored the themes: God is kind, Jesus is kind, and Spirit is kind.[103] This chapter gathers the material in a focused way for a new understanding of the trinity.

Some theologians have said that since the church has sanctioned the doctrine of the trinity and added Trinity Sunday as a part of the Christian lectionary we should not meddle with it. Having served as a minister in churches for

---

[101] Ralph Waldo Emerson.

[102] See my book, *A Center That Holds: An Adventure in Kindness*, for more on the transforming power of centering on kindness and the gifts that kindness brings to the worshiping community.

[103] These chapters are similar to the ones in *A Center That Holds*. They have been rewritten, using more biblical insights and new ways of seeing these teachings through the lens of process theology, to bring out more of the trinitarian relationships.

over fifty years, I have a deep love and appreciation for the church; however, the history of the church is filled with bad choices like the sanctioning of slavery, using sexist language, and approving of wars. The traditional trinitarian statements of Father, Son, and Holy Spirit have been seen as promoting patriarchal and sexist language that barred women from Christian ordained ministry. The church is always in need of transformation.

My use of the metaphor, kindness, as a process hermeneutic for interpreting the biblical message challenges the exclusive language of the traditional trinity and presents a new doctrine that seeks to show how God relates to the people of God, first in the Scriptures and also to us. For me, kindness expresses this relationship best.[104]

Kindness as used in the Old Testament is a key metaphor for the way the Jewish people experienced God. Exodus 33:19 defines God as kindness in this foundational "I am" saying. "I am God, and I show mercy and kindness to anyone I choose."[105] This verse names God as Kindness. So what the Christian belief in the trinity names as God the Father is best conceived as "God is kind." Kindness is a gender neutral term and does not alienate like the name Father does for some who have been forsaken or abused by

---

[104] See *Trinity in Process: A Relational Theology of God*. Eds. Joseph A. Bracken, S.J. and Marjorie Hewitt Suchocki for a history of these trinitarian challenges and other fresh ways of seeing the trinity from a process philosophy perspective. My book is based more on the Bible and the teachings of Jesus.

[105] Contemporary English Version of the Bible.

their earthly father. The previous chapters have amply shown this reality of kindness. The faith of Israel can be stated in these three words: God is kind. As we have seen, the Psalms of Israel are filled with the "loving kindness" of God. This first part of the trinity can be stated as "I believe God is kind to all living things."

Kindness is also an appropriate metaphor for expressing what is intended in the second part of the Christian trinity: the Son. Paul expressed the birth of Jesus in these words: "When the kindness of God came, God saved us."[106] Jesus' self-designation was "I am kind."[107] Self- designations should carry more importance than titles we apply to Jesus. The second part of the trinity can be stated as "I believe Jesus is kind and calls us to be kind to one another."

Why do we speak of God's kindness revealed in Jesus' tender teachings? In Galilee God met Jesus with tenderness and Jesus became totally God-conscious, self-actualizing the glory of God in his life; and, thus, became a bridge between earthly and heavenly glories. The depth of his relationship to God was the uniqueness of his life and ministry. Jesus revealed this relationship by addressing God as a child would talk to a parent. Jesus who was like a Son and God who was like a Father met each rising occasion in the life of his disciples with tenderness and thereby they are drawn into this centering faith stamped with heavenly activity and glory. John described this as the glory of Jesus: "The word

---

[106] Titus 3:4.

[107] Matthew 11:28-30.

(λογος), the creative principle and the wisdom of God (σοφια), were self-actualized in Jesus; and Jesus, full of kindness and truth, lived among us. We saw his glory, the glory which he received as the Father's Son."[108]

Jesus' prayer in John, chapter seventeen, reveals even more the depth of this kind relationship to God: "Father, the hour has come; glorify your Son, so that the Son may glorify you."[109] This prayer should be called the "Lord's Prayer" and the one we call the "Lord's Prayer" should be called the disciple's prayer. The disciples were the recipients of this glory: "I give them the same glory you gave me, so that they may be one, just as you and I are one."[110] The disciples in turn are to go out and meet each rising occasion in their ministry with tenderness, reflecting this glory of God's tenderness to the world: "My glory is shown through them."[111] As one who embodied this glory, Jesus became a heavenly messenger who acts out of his oneness with God. How does this fit with Jesus' lowly ministry in Galilee as seen in Mark? We might speak of this as a lowliness hidden in glory.

It is probably accurate to say that lowliness and glory, humiliation and exaltation, are not separated in Jesus' life and ministry like two stages on a journey---his lowliness seen in Galilee and his exaltation in Jerusalem. They are

---

[108] Based on John 1:14.

[109] John 17:1, NRSV.

[110] John 17:22.

[111] John 17:10.

rather united with each other at all times in Jesus' life. If, indeed, the Temple visit at the age of twelve is an indication, Jesus was aware at that point of his unity with God. His response to his mother was, "I must be about my Father's business."[112] We have to remember that the Gospels were written from the end backward to the beginning; and they were written about forty to seventy years after the crucifixion and resurrection of Jesus. As happens with any important person, in the writing they take on mythic and legendary characteristics. The Temple visit is an example. Luke the Gospel writer is known as a historian and gave attention to detail, and this can be seen in the story, giving it an historical kernel.

At least from the time of his baptism onward, Jesus' union with God is evident: "As soon as Jesus came up out of the water, he saw heaven opening and the Spirit coming down on him like a dove. And a voice came from heaven, "You are my Son. I am pleased with you.""[113]

The earthly Jesus who goes forth into a world of suffering and death does not lose his sense of oneness with God. Instead, he dies with this awareness on his lips: "Father, in your hands I place my spirit!"[114] Jesus' total commitment to God's aims is his glory, and this glory shone on the face of Jesus all through his gentle Galilean ministry. The Gospel

---

[112] Luke 2:49.

[113] Mark 1:10-11.

[114] Luke 23:46.

of John seems to have substituted the "glory of God" for Mark, Matthew, and Luke's use of the "Kingdom of God."

As the worthy model of all humanity, God raised Jesus to heaven where he comes before the throne of God and becomes as one with God and the saints around the throne. In Spirit Jesus returns to earth where he encourages his followers in continuing his gentle ministry and tender teachings. Much of the New Testament virtually equates Spirit and the risen Jesus,[115] seeing their role as one as in the Gospel of John, chapter 14. When discussing God, Jesus, and Spirit we are talking about mystery filled relationships. Using kindness as a metaphor makes these relationships as clear as possible. Kindness certainly communicates better with children than the title, Holy Spirit, which can be a spooky title to a young child. Spirit is best equated with the risen Jesus. The third part of the trinity can be stated as "I believe Spirit is the Risen Jesus continuing kind teachings in the church, his new body."

The Bible does not teach that there are three Gods. The Old and New Testaments profess that "The Lord our God is One."[116] This is the one non-negotiable truth in any discussion of the trinity. The Christian Church has not done very well in explaining the trinity so as to maintain the oneness of God. It is time for starting over with new and fresh meanings. I find these words from Emerson challenging: "Do not follow where the path may lead. Go,

[115] See the last chapter on Spirit is Kind.

[116] Deuteronomy 6:4; Mark 12:29.

instead, where there is no path and leave a trail." I believe one way of fulfilling this wise advice is to mark a new trail to trinitarian truths. Perhaps, making Kindness our new trinity will leave in its tracks the markings of this new trail:

I believe God is kind to all living things.

I believe Jesus is kind and calls us to be kind.

I believe Spirit is Jesus alive in the Church teaching kindness.

Concluding Meditative Thought: The One God has chosen to relate to us as kindness in Jesus' tender teachings and as Spirit in the continuing ministry of the church. Relational terms do not capture all of the greatness of God, but they do help us understand God better. The New Testament writers show a lot of diversity in the way they present the good news. John in Revelation especially has shown great freedom in his apocalyptic vision of the new heaven and new earth. His freedom and the freedom of all New Testament writers to reshape the Jesus tradition invite us to look for new images as well. Soon after the New Testament was written church leaders started trying to explain the ways God relates to us and the world. This search should never stop. In fact, the church should be like a crustacean shedding its theological skin every few years so that it can grow a new one. Can you think of new images to express how God relates to us?

How would you flesh out my three trinitarian statements? I believe God is kind to all living things. I believe Jesus is kind and calls us to be kind. I believe the Spirit is Jesus alive in the church teaching kindness. With the guidance of your minister you might want to start a discussion group in your church to explore this possibility of a new understanding of the trinity. I have purposively not encumbered this book with the history of the trinitarian problems. This is a well-documented history.[117] What we need is not restatement but

---

[117] I appreciate the struggle of the early church in trying to show how Jesus incarnated God and how God's Spirit continued to inspire the church after Jesus' death and resurrection. However, the church leaders went too far in speaking of three persons that led to belief in three Gods. Our doctrine of the trinity has been developed around the biblical theme

reinterpretation using fresh images. You might ask your minister to guide you through this history or perhaps he or she could invite a retired minister to help guide your discussion group as you explore new images. Trained theologians and professors of religious history may be better able to understand the trinity of the past, but lay persons using art, poetry, music and daily experiences are often better equipped to put these teachings in fresh new ideas that communicate today.

Give it a try.

---

of monotheism, using kindness to express the relational aspects of God seen in Jesus and his continuing presence in Spirit empowered gentle teachings.

Trinity-The Way We Experience God[118]

"Jesus' eleven disciples went to a mountain in Galilee, where Jesus had told them to meet him. They saw him and worshipped him, but some of them doubted. Then Jesus came to them and said: I have been given all authority in heaven and on earth! Go to the people of all nations and make them my disciples. Baptize them in the name of the Father, the Son, and the Holy Spirit, and teach them to do everything I have told you. I will be with you always, even to the end of the world."[119]

An elderly man took his ugly looking dog for his regular Sunday walk in the park. The man stopped at a park bench to rest, and his dog played at his feet. Soon another man appeared with his dog. The younger man's face had taken on the mean look of his bulldog, and they both were itching for a fight. The younger man began to taunt the older man and his ugly dog. He commanded his dog, "Spike," and pointed at the ugly dog. The older man calmly said, "I wouldn't do that if I were you." This only irritated the younger man, and he commanded Spike to attack the ugly dog. The older man reiterated, "I wouldn't have done that!" The battle raged in cartoon fashion with barking and hair flying. The result was unexpected. Spike lay defeated by the ugly dog. His humbled master said to the older man, "I am

---

[118] This sermon and the following one in the next chapter are given to show how a doctrine of the trinity may be preached and celebrated in the church.

[119] Matthew 28:18-20, CEV.

impressed. What kind of dog is that anyway?" The older man replied, "Well, before I cut off his tail and painted him yellow, he was an alligator!"

Things are not always as they appear. Situations are easily misread. This is especially true of the Bible that was written over a period of a thousand years and contains 66 different books in the Protestant Bible and 73 in the Roman Catholic Bible. The Bible is used to support the handling of snakes and the drinking of poison as a test of one's faith in God. Some in Bible days saw Jesus as a drunkard and some even thought that Jesus was demon possessed, others saw him as the Son of God. Our views of God are often confused. The prophet Isaiah said, God's ways are not our ways and God's thoughts are not our thoughts!

Yet, there is an essential unity in the Bible. God relates to us in saving ways and that is the meaning of the trinity. The non-biblical word, trinity, is a word coined by theologians to explain the way God relates to the world and the way Christians experience God. After experiencing the life, teachings, death, and resurrection of Jesus, Matthew closes his Gospel with this quote from the risen Jesus: "All authority in heaven and on earth has been given to me. Go therefore and make disciples of all nations, baptizing them in the name of the Father, and of the Son, and of the Holy Spirit, and teaching them to obey everything that I have commanded you. And remember, I am with you always, to the end of the age."[120]

From beginning to end this passage from the Gospel of Matthew is about God relating to the world and how people of the world experience God in saving ways. Matthew testified to what he had experienced in Jesus. He described his experience of God in relational terms, as Father, Son, and Holy Spirit. These verses speak of experiencing God in three distinct relational ways, and our theology is best described as a relational theology. First, God the Father nurtures all things to fullness, goodness, and love. God meets each rising entity with tenderness, desiring to share goodness and love with the world in relational ways. From the beginning God wanted the world to be like a beautiful garden where everyone related to each other in love and harmony. Love does not force or coerce to get its way. Love grants freedom of choice and creates a climate of freedom. Instead of relating to God and each other in love, humans exercised their freedom of choice and rebelled against God and struck out at each other. In these mythic stories representing all humanity the first family is broken by sin. Cain even murdered his own brother, Abel, out of jealousy.

Yet, God did not give up. Like a good gardener, God nurtured a special relationship of loving kindness with Israel and formed a covenant of faith with Israel. God knew how the seed faith should grow and what it should produce. God

---

[120] Matthew 28:18-20, NRSV. This key trinitarian passage was read in the worship service by an elder. It is repeated here in the sermon from another version of the Bible.

the gardener knew how much sun, water, and nutrients were needed to produce fruit. In loving kindness God took care of Israel. God gave her the law through Moses and spoke tenderly to her in the prophets. In all of these ways God related to Israel like farmer Green Jeans tenderly caring for the family garden.

Israel at times responded beautifully and at other times rebelled and failed to shine as a light to the nations. So, God, who spoke the beautiful garden into existence, chose a second relational path. Jesus' response to the call of God in his life and ministry made it possible for God to walk in the garden in human form. The Word that spoke creation into existence became flesh in Jesus' response to God's call and lived in the garden world. As Jesus actualized God's presence, God now relates to the world in saving ways in Jesus, walking with us along the paths of life. When our son, Kevin was in Church preschool, I was walking home with him for lunch one day. I was caught up in the sermon I had been working on and was walking too fast for 4 year old Kevin. He yelled, "Daddy, slow down. Take little short steps so I can keep up with you." I turned back, scooped him up, and carried him the rest of the way home. In Jesus' faithful response to God's call, God came to walk with us. God picks us up and carries us when we need to be helped. In walking with us in Jesus, God does not cease to be God. God is greater than God revealed in Jesus.

In announcing Jesus's birth Matthew wrote, "You shall call him Jesus, for he will save his people from their sins."[121] An explanation of the name, Jesus, is added--- and they shall name him Emmanuel, which means, God is with us.[122] The message is clear: God is present in Jesus! And this is the meaning of the trinity!

Jesus modeled tender loving care. In the rainy season, parts of Galilee, where Jesus performed most of his ministry, were like a garden. So, Jesus pointed to the flowers and said, "Consider the lilies of the field, how they grow; they neither toil nor spin, yet I tell you, even Solomon in all his glory was not clothed like one of these. If God so clothes the grass of the field . . . will he not much more care for you."[123]

In his creative responsive acts of love, Jesus gave a face to God. The disciples looked at Jesus and saw the glory of God in Jesus.[124] If you look at a picture of my daughter at age 12 and a picture of me at the same age, we look like identical twins. My daughter looks at me today and has nightmares about this genetic likeness; it doesn't bode well for her looks in the future.

In many ways the disciples saw God in Jesus. Phillip wanted to see more of God, and in the upper room he asked Jesus to show him God. Jesus replied, Philip, have I been with

---

[121] Matthew 1:21.

[122] Matthew 1:23.

[123] Matthew 6:28-29, NRSV.

[124] John 1:14.

you all this time and you still do not know me? Whoever has seen me has seen God. How can you say, "Show us God?" Do you not believe that God and I are one?[125] Jesus gave a physical face to God, and that face is kindness. They did not see two separate faces. In the face of the human Jesus, God's spiritual face shines bright; and it shines upon us as we turn our face toward Jesus and look full in his wonderful face. Everything in the countenance of Jesus reveals God. However, God is greater than God revealed in Jesus. This is the glory of Jesus and the glory of God. And this is the meaning of the trinity!

As wonderful as this new relational activity of God in Jesus is for the early Christian community, there is a new transformation that occurs with the resurrection of Jesus. As the cross became immanent, Jesus made a wonderful promise: "I am sending you the Spirit who will keep on living in you."[126] Spirit is the third way God relates to us. Spirit is one with God and one with the risen Jesus. Jesus said that my Spirit will live in you. A wonderful transformation occurs here. Now the followers of Jesus give a face to Spirit, to Jesus, and to God. God has no other physical face than what is seen in the people of God. Where the people of God accurately reflect the life of Jesus, God has many friendly faces and encouraging faces; and they are all the face of God. The presence of God in Jesus made it possible for God to be present in all persons. God transformed in the Risen Jesus and incarnated in the people

---

[125] John 14:8-10.

[126] John 14:17.

87

of God is without limits. God is now relating to people who open their lives to Spiritual Presence in all times and places. The Risen Jesus makes this promise in these comforting words: I am with you always, even to the end of the ages.[127] And this is the meaning of the trinity!

The heart of all these teachings is saving kindness. God's loving kindness is in the world meeting each rising occasion with tenderness. Jesus self-actualized the kindness of God in his tender teachings. The Risen Jesus as Spirit enables us to share this loving kindness with others. So, the one constant is unconditional love and kindness. The face of God is revealed as creative responsive kindness, and we form our theology of evangelism around these relational truths. What are the implications of this understanding of the trinity as creative responsive kindness? Individuals may relate to God and experience God in different cultures and different religions. Wherever people come to God in kindness there is salvation. The Jewish person who comes to God through the Old Testament Scriptures experiences the loving kindness of God as surely as the Christian who experiences the kindness of God through Jesus. The one true God is revealed in Jesus, but not only in Jesus. God is greater than God revealed in Jesus. History would have been written differently if the church had only seen this relational truth about God. All the hatred between Jews and Christians would be erased. All the rivalry between different religions would be useless. Racial hatred and gender battles would be eliminated. Kindness is the great equalizer.

---

[127] Matthew 28:20.

Christians could still witness in a spirit of love to the uniqueness of Jesus, without being judgmental of others who experience a deep tender love of God in their faith experience.

The face of God, Jesus, and Spirit is One. The most central teaching of the Old and New Testaments is this: Hear, O Israel, the Lord, our God, is one Lord. The Spirit of God draws us to salvation. We relate to God as Creative Spirit who spoke all things into existence. We relate to God as Jesus who made the kindness of God tangible in human form.[128] And, we relate to God as the Risen Jesus who is still active in reconciling the whole universe in saving ways. The Risen Jesus is also known as Spirit who is in all believers as Friend, Helper, and Comforter. These are all relational ways we experience God and God experiences us. And this is the meaning of the trinity!

The mystery of these relational trinitarian truths becomes most meaningful to us in our experience of suffering and evil. This was certainly true for Mother Teresa. This dynamic nun was barely over four feet tall, but she radiated with God's love and kindness. She went out in the streets of Calcutta each morning and tenderly picked up the unwanted babies and the elderly who were placed on the streets to die. She inspired others to do the same and a clinic was started, later others were added around the world. When an interviewer told Mother Teresa that she was doing a great work with the poor in Calcutta, she fiddled with her hands

---

[128] See I John 1:1-3.

like a little child, and said, "It is Jesus really." It was a short interview, but long on meaning. "It is Jesus." Mother Teresa did not pretend to solve the mystery of suffering. But by bringing the poor into her heart, she brought them to the heart of God. Her face had become the face of God for the poor. Mother Teresa knew that suffering and redemption had something to do with Jesus and the power of Spirit. Indeed, her work was the work of God revealed in Jesus and empowered by Spirit.

Does anyone see Jesus in you? Can you say of your work, "It is Jesus?" If people say, "You taught a good Sunday School Class," is your reply---"It is Jesus!" After I preach a sermon, can I say, "It is Jesus?" If we encounter needy individuals, do we see Jesus in them? When we reach that point, we can say that we understand the Trinity. Until we reach that level of maturity, we continue to worship in mystery and pray---

Lord, my heart is not large enough,

My memory is not good enough,

My will is not strong enough:

Take my heart and enlarge it.

Take my memory and give it quicker recall.

Take my will and make it strong

And make me conscious of thee, ever present,

ever accompanying.[129]

Glory be to the Maker of heaven and earth who comes to us in saving ways in Jesus and empowering ways in Spirit, our Friend and Helper. May the ever-present God be with you!

---

[129] *The Oxford Book of Prayer.*

Why Do We Celebrate Trinity Sunday Anyway?

*"I have much more to say to you, but right now it would be more than you could understand. **The Spirit shows what is true and will come and guide you into the full truth.** The Spirit doesn't speak on his own. He will tell you only what he has heard from me, and he will let you know what is going to happen. The Spirit will bring glory to me by taking my message and telling it to you. Everything that the Father has is mine. That is why I have said that the Spirit takes my message and tells it to you."*[130]

You and I live in a world where horrible things can and do happen. Accidents, illness, and death can come without rhyme or reason. At such times we confront the reality of the chaotic in God's good creation. In such moments it is comforting to know that the bad is contained in the boundaries of God's beautiful and good creation.

A mother who lost a teenage son in an automobile accident described how on the morning of the funeral she rose early and read in Job the speeches of God from the whirlwind (chapters. 38-42). When asked why she chose these chapters from Job, she replied, "I needed to know that my pain was not all there was in the world." Like Job, her pain was so deep that it threatened to swallow all of her life. What she needed was to know that God's power as creator and

---

[130] John 16:12-15, CEV. Read also Proverbs 8:1-4, 20-36.

redeemer was greater than her pain. Hearing the words of how God established the world on secure foundations, the return of the morning sun each day to light the earth, the life giving water, and the nurture of the animals was reassuring in spite of her loss and pain. God's creation supports and sustains life. This woman, like all who suffer, learned that God was there, and in being there God could share her pain.

It is this experience of God's presence with us and for us that we seek in celebrating Trinity Sunday. Churches have been celebrating Trinity Sunday since the Middle Ages. On this day the church celebrates the fullness of God's relationship with God's people. If this sounds like a difficult and uninviting topic, don't tune out just yet. In fact, the whole Christian Gospel may just be contained in this doctrine of the trinity.

In a few short verses the Gospel of John gives us a good reason to celebrate Trinity Sunday: "The Spirit shows what is true and will come and guide you into the full truth. The Spirit doesn't speak on his own. He will tell you only what he has heard from me, and he will let you know what is going to happen. The Spirit will bring glory to me by taking my message and telling it to you. Everything that the Father has is mine. That is why I have said that the Spirit takes my message and tells it to you."

The Bible speaks of the kindness of God, the kindness of Jesus, and the kindness of Spirit in ways that inspire wonder and mystery and seeks understanding of these relationships. Yet, like all words used to describe God, the word, trinity,

93

is inadequate. A sense of mystery is at the heart of the Christian experience of God, for no mortal can comprehend the immortal God. The very idea of the Eternal God who called creation out of chaos over billions of years relating to us mortals as a caring Parent, as saving love in Jesus, and as an empowering Spiritual Friend, is mind boggling. Yet, this mysterious truth is what Christians celebrate on Trinity Sunday!

So, let me invite you into the mystery. The key word for unlocking the door into the mystery of the trinity is the word, relationship. The Bible is about relationships: God relating to us and us relating to God. In relational terms, Jesus sets us on the right path in studying the trinity, and indeed, the whole Gospel, when he said that the first commandment is Listen, Israel! The Lord our God is One. Love the Lord your God with all your heart, with all your soul, with all your mind, and with all your strength.[131]

So, how does the word, relationship, help to understand trinitarian aspects of God? The Bible speaks of God relating to us in a three-fold way: as a Parent, as a Son, and as Spirit. Yet, it is the One God who relates in these three ways. Jesus himself said, The Lord our God is One!

Let me use a human analogy. As one person, I am a father; I have a daughter and a son. I am a son; my parents were Robert and Jessie Cole. I am a spirit. Now don't get spooked! I know I am straining the analogy a bit; I can be

---

[131] Mark 12:29-30.

present to others in a spiritual, i.e., non-temporal and non-spatial way. When our daughter, Kimberly, was in medical school in Denver, Colorado and our son, Kevin, was in graduate school at Berkeley, what Beth and I taught them at home was with them there. We were a source of strength for them in their lives. In one sense, I was with them there, in another time and place from the time and place I was in at home. Also, I say to people going into hospital, "I will be praying for you," or "I will be with you." People gain strength from that knowledge. So, at one and the same time I can relate as a father, a son, and a presence.[132] Yet, I remain one person. How much more this is true of God!

The One God has chosen to relate to us as a loving Parent, a saving Son, and an enabling Friend. These relational terms do not capture all of the greatness of God, but they do help us understand God better.

With these relational terms firmly in mind, let us now consider our title for this chapter: Why do we celebrate Trinity Sunday anyway? Why do we spend time with these old Scriptures? I would suggest this reason for your consideration: In the midst of a world of evil and suffering, where sons and daughters do die in terrible accidents, it is good to know that there is a God who is like a kind Father and nurturing Mother, a Parent God, if you will, who creates a good and beautiful world for our enjoyment. This God

---

[132] Obviously this analogy is inadequate. It is used solely to express relationship not essence or other trinitarian terms that have been used in the past. Its strength is that I remained one and the same person in all of the relationships. Maintaining the oneness of God in trinitarian discussions is essential.

chose not to remain apart from the world, but became present in the world in the prophets, psalmists, and in Jesus' tender teachings in saving ways to bring the gift of abundant life to us. In accepting this gift we gain Shalom---wholeness and peace. This relational Parent God remains with us as an empowering Friend to pervade our universe and be in our lives to console, comfort, and encourage us so that we may know that life is good. Indeed, in the words of Genesis, It is very good! God is on the side of life and its joyous fulfillment! In other words, no matter what evil may say, God is for us! This is what the mother was seeking on the day of the funeral for her son, and this is the message that needs to be proclaimed in all trinitarian discussions.

So, why do we celebrate Trinity Sunday? Life is good, and we have much to celebrate. Holding on to this truth instills in us optimism, confidence, and a sense of wellbeing in spite of evil and suffering. We simply need to take time to be graced by those serene moments of beauty that are a part of our good creation.

Psalms, chapter 8, leads us into that spirit with a hymn of praise to God's glory: O Lord, our Lord, your greatness is seen in the world. Proverbs, chapter 8, goes even further in its spirit of joyful celebration of God's beautiful and good creation. Lady Wisdom is the speaker: I was there before God began to create the earth. At the very first the Lord gave life to me. . . . I was there when the Lord put the heavens in place and stretched the sky over the surface of the sea. I was with him when he placed the clouds in the sky and created the springs that fill the ocean. I was there when he set boundaries for the sea to make it obey him, and when he laid the foundations to support the earth. I was beside the Lord, helping him plan and build. I made him happy each day, and I was happy at his side. I was pleased with his world and pleased with its people. Pay attention, my children! Follow my advice, and you will be happy. . . .By finding me, you find life, and the Lord will be pleased with you.[133]

This wisdom hymn presents life as a joyous dance with God. Sophia (Wisdom), says, I was happy at God's side, and God was happy that I was there.[134] For this biblical writer, God is a relational God! God provides a good and beautiful world for our enjoyment. What causes you to break out in praise like the Psalmist and Sophia?

I have harvested some special moments in God's good and beautiful creation and stored them in my memory bank. They are a part of the calm center out of which I live. One morning Beth and I sat on top of Clingmans Dome in the Great Smokey Mountains, before pollution began to kill some of the trees, and looked at the mist from the valleys below. We took in the pristine, majestic view of the Smokies; and, as we did so, we felt a divine presence with us. In these moments we were relating with God and a friendly universe.

On another day we sat on the lip of the Grand Canyon and looked out across the chasm at the changing hues and colors

---

[133] Proverbs 8, CEV.

[134] Proverbs 8:30.

of the rainbow. Again we felt a Spiritual Friend with us, and we knew that life is good and beautiful. We felt a little like we were dancing with God.

My favorite place in this friendly, good, and beautiful creation is Hatteras Island and the Outer Banks of North Carolina when the sun peeks over the Atlantic Ocean. I enjoy standing in the surf and catching a speckled trout or flounder. That is a spine-tingling experience for me. In those moments I see the greatness of God and I feel close to God who is like a good Parent providing good and beautiful things for children to enjoy!

What are your memories? I encourage you to harvest such moments and store them in your memory bank. Does living in God's good earth make you want to sing with the Psalmist, O God, your greatness is seen in all the world?

We hold these memories in our hearts and souls. Lest we forget, we have to relive and re-experience them ever so often. Even so, lest we forget, we need to celebrate the stories of our faith. Trinity Sunday gathers up the fundamental truths of our faith:

I believe God is kind to all living things.

I believe Jesus is kind and calls us to be kind.

I believe Spirit is Jesus alive in the Church teaching kindness.

In confessing these core beliefs, we reorganize and energize our lives around them.[135] And in remembering these core truths, evil is not any less real, but seen from this broad perspective of life's goodness and beauty, evil's power over us is diminished, if not totally eradicated!

The real purpose of these trinitarian truths is to draw us into the presence of our loving God where we may offer our aches and anxieties to God. When we come to God, we are enfolded in caring arms and we know everything will be all right.

It's like a conversation between a husband and wife where the man is rattling on about all that is wrong and not listening to his wife until she says, "Did you hear what I said?" The man replies, "No." And the woman says, "I love you!" He says, "Oh!" And it is like the sun shining through dark clouds. Jesus is that sunshine breaking through the clouds and saying, "I love you."

Loving and Kind God, we praise you for the beauty and goodness of creation which inspires our vision of reality and enables us to live victoriously in an evil age. Through saving love you make us whole and become our Empowering Friend. Fill us with the vision of your glory, that we may always praise you and serve you in kind thoughts and actions. Amen.

---

135 See my book, *A Center that Holds: Adventures in Kindness.*

Conclusion

Historically Christians have had difficulty understanding and explaining how God, clothed in mystery, is present in the world and in our lives. Christian theologians have also had difficulty with the non-biblical term, trinity, from the beginning, and it has not served the church very well. For the average person in the church pew, the word, trinity, evokes the image of three Gods: Father, Son, and Holy Spirit. The Bible never intended this belief in three Gods. The one non-negotiable tenet for the Bible is **monotheism**, the belief in one God; and this has been the central motif throughout this book. The Shema, the central creed of both The Old and New Testaments, is this:

> *"The Lord our God is the only true God! So love the Lord your God with all your heart, soul, and strength."*
> (Deuteronomy 6:4-5, CEV)

The purpose of this book has been not to retell the history of the trinity, but to present the word, kindness, as a rich new metaphor for understanding the relational purpose of the trinity. I have shown how kindness is a theme throughout the scriptures, and that the biblical writers gave the name, kindness, to God, to Jesus, and to Spirit. To be sure, the kind spirit of the biblical writers was often in tension with feelings of anger, wrath, hate, and vengeance. These human

100

negative emotions were fueled in times of captivity and intense persecution and often attributed to God.

In making kindness my hermeneutic for interpreting the trinity and all the scriptures, I recognize that I am packing a lot of meaning in this one word, kindness. By giving God, Jesus, and Spirit the name, Kindness, I have given the term creative, redeeming, and sanctifying qualities. And in using kindness as an umbrella like term, it has drawn other rich words like love, mercy, and grace into its healing energies.

So the real question for further study may be, Why encumber the word, kindness, a rich biblical and culturally contagious word, with the word, trinity that carries a lot of baggage? In a quest for a moral compass and a global ethic for our troubled world, some carry this question further and ask, "Why speak of God, Jesus, and Spirit at all?"[136] Do we need the Bible to have a moral compass? Why not just use the word, kindness?

Monotheistic religions have tended to see morality and ethics as a set system of truth revealed in the Bible. This view is challenged by atheists, humanism, and those who have surveyed the history of moral thought. Confucianism has built a strong moral Chinese society without reference to God. Buddhism also builds a strong ethical way of life without the need for God.[137] When one adds to this moral societal history the abusive practices like slavery, sexist

---

[136] Kenan Malik raises this very question in his book, *The Quest for a Moral Compass: A Global History of Ethics.*

[137] Ibid. p.339.

attitudes that contribute to abuse and violence, and the sanctioning of war that is often supported by biblical proof-texting, one can see the need for transformation.

This has been the maze through which this book has sought to mark a new pathway. From my experience I have found that the word, kindness, is the best word to use for finding a new path to morality and ethics. I affirm that secular humanists and world religions like Buddhism can help build a moral and ethical society. Yet, for me, using kindness wedded to the fullest revelation of God seen in the Spirt inspired gentle teachings and actions of Jesus provides the best path to transforming society and finding peace in our global age. This hermeneutic of kindness brings transforming love energies in its wake.

From the Bible, we know God revealed in the prophets and in Jesus as a uniquely personal and relational God, best described as creative responsive kindness. Jesus' gentle teachings especially capture this central truth about God: God is kind. As the creative impulse and adventurous energy that gives value to all of life, God is mystery. Yet God is present in the coming into being of all things. God calls all things into existence and tenderly guides and nurtures all things through the ages.

Seeking morality and ethics apart from this biblical faith perspective loses this healing transforming energy. Also, just traveling the way of kindness alone, apart from the hermeneutic of Jesus' tender teachings strips kindness of its richness. Kindness can be shallow and self-serving. Jesus' kind teachings and actions as the actualization of God's kindness, give a richness based on two thousand years of covenantal history in which God is in the world and for the world, in us and for us in transforming energy.

Kindness is an adventurous path with new discoveries being made every day. An example is a documentary by David Gaz (2015), *Kindness is Contagious*, narrated by Catherine Ryan Hyde, the author of the novel and film, *Pay It Forward*. This documentary beautifully shows how small acts of kindness can spread rapidly as each recipient of kindness shares kindness with others.[138] So, let us go and be kind to one another. We may not be able to give all the kindness the world needs, but the world needs all the kindness we can give!

---

[138] One person interviewed in the documentary, Kindness is Contagious, is Dacher Keltner, professor of psychology at the University of California, Berkeley, and director of the Good Science Center. His book, *Born to Be Good*, supports my thesis of kindness as an evolutionary principle.

Meditation

Think of a time someone was kind to you and you extended that kindness to another person. Parents can share stories of kindness with their children and observe how it affects the child's actions with others. I have observed that grandparents can especially affect the attitude and actions of their grandchildren. Try to observe and note this in your extended family, if possible.

Bibliography

Adams, Edward. *Parallel Lives of Jesus: A Guide to the Four Gospels.* Louisville: Westminster/John Knox, 2011.

Allison, Dale C. *Constructing Jesus: Memory, Imagination, and History.* Grand Rapids: Baker, 2011.

Armstrong, Karen. *The Great Transformation.* New York: Anchor, 2006

Aslan, Reza. *Zealot.* New York: Random House. 2013.

Bauckham, Richard. *The Theology of the Book of Revelation.* New Testament Theology. Cambridge: Cambridge University Press, 1993.

Beale, G. K. *The Book of Revelation: A Commentary on the Greek Text.* The New International Greek Testament Commentary. Grand Rapids: Eerdmans, 2013.

Berry, Wendell. *The Gift of Good Land.* San Francisco: North Point Press, 1981.

Borg, Marcus J. *Jesus: A New Vision.* New York: Harper Collins, 1991.

Bornkamm, Gunther. *Jesus of Nazareth.* Trans. Irene and Fraser McLuskey with James M. Robinson. New York: Harper & Row, Publishers, 1960.

Boyd, Gregory. *Trinity and Process: A Critical Evaluation and Reconstruction of Hartshorne"s Di-Polar Theism towards a Trinitarian Metaphysics.* New York: Peter Lang, 1992.

Bracken, Joseph A. S.J. *The Triune Symbol: Persons, Process, and Community.* Lanham, MD: University Press of America, 1985.

_____. Society and Spirit: *A Trinitarian Cosmology.* Cranbury, NJ: Associated University Presses, 1991.

_____and Marjorie Hewitt Suchocki, ed. *Trinity in Process: A Relational Theology of God.* New York: Continuum Publishing Co., 1997.

Bultmann, Rudolph. *Jesus and the Word.* Trans. Louise Pettibone Smith and Erminie Huntress Lantero. New York: Charles Scribner's Sons, 1958.

Burrows, Millar. *Jesus in the First Three Gospels.* Nashville: Abingdon, 1977.

Carson, Rachel. *The Sense of Wonder.* New York: Harper & Row, 1987.

Cobb, John B. Jr. *Becoming a Thinking Christian.* Nashville: Abingdon Press, 1993.

_____. *Christ in a Pluralistic Age.* Eugene, Or: Wipf and Stock Publishers, 1998.

_____. *God and the World.* Philadelphia: Westminster Press, 1969.

_____. *Lay Theology*. St. Louis: Chalice Press, 1994.

_____ and David Ray Griffin. *Process Theology: An Introductory Exposition*. Philadelphia: Westminster Press, 1976.

Cole, Dwayne. *A Center that Holds: Adventures in Kindness*. Cleveland, Tennessee: Parson's Porch Books, 2015.

_____. *A Prayer of Blessing: As You Go Remember This*. Cleveland, Tennessee: Parson's Porch Books, 2015.

_____. *Jesus' Transforming Beatitudes: Selected Sermons for Year A*. Cleveland, Tennessee: Parson's Porch Books, 2015.

_____. *Jesus' Transforming Love: Selected Sermons for Year B*. Cleveland, Tennessee: Parson's Porch Books, 2014.

_____. *Jesus' Transforming Gentle Teachings: Selected Sermons for Year C*. Cleveland, Tennessee: Parson's Porch Books, 2015.

_____. *The Apostles' Creed: A Living Creed for the Living Church*. Cleveland, Tennessee: Parson's Porch Books, 2014.

_____. *The Book of Revelation: Jesus' Kindness Transforms Suffering*. Cleveland, Tennessee: Parson's Porch Books, 2015.

_____. *The Serenity Prayer: A Pathway to Peace and Happiness*. Cleveland, Tennessee: Parson's Porch Books, 2015.

_____. *The Story of the Bible: Its Authority, Inspiration, Canonization, and Translation*. Cleveland, Tennessee: Parson's Porch Books, 2015.

Cullman, Oscar. *Christology of the New Testament*. Philadelphia: Westminster Press, 1963.

Daley, B. *The Hope of the Early Church*. Cambridge: Cambridge University Press, 1991.

Darwin, Charles. *The Descent of Man*. New York: Modern Library, 1977

Ehrman, Bart D. *How Jesus Became God*. New York: Harper Collins Publishers, 2014.

Feuillet, A. *The Apocalypse*. Trans. T. E. Crane. New York: Alba House, 1965.

Ferrucci, Piero. *The Power of Kindness*. New York: Penguin Group, 2006.

Ford, Lewis S. *The Lure of God: A Biblical Background for Process Theism*. Philadelphia: Fortress Press. 1978.

_____. *Transforming Process Theism*. Albany: State University Press. 2000.

Frankl, Viktor E. *Man's Search for Meaning: An Introduction to Logotherapy*. Third Edition. New York: Simon & Schuster, 1984.

_____. *The Will to Meaning: Foundations and Applications of Logotherapy*. Expanded Edition. New York: Meridian, 1988.

Fromm, Erich. *The Art of Loving*. New York: Harper & Row, 1989.

Fuller, Reginald H. *The Foundations of New Testament Christology*. New York: Charles Scribner's Sons, 1955.

Funk, Robert W. *The Acts of Jesus: The Search for the Authentic Deeds of Jesus*. San Francisco: Harper Collins, 1998.

Funk, Robert W. and Roy W. Hoover. *The Jesus Seminar*, 1993. *The Five Gospels: The Search for the Authentic Words of Jesus*. New York: Macmillan, Polebridge Press. 1993.

Good, Deirdre J. *Jesus the Meek King*. Harrisburg: Trinity Press, 1999.

Hartshorne, Charles. *The Divine Relativity*. New Haven: Yale University Press, 1948.

Heacox, Kim. *John Muir: And The Ice That Started A Fire*. Guilford, Connecticut: Lyons Press, 2014.

Horsley, Richard, and John S. Hanson. *Galilee: History, Politics, People*. Pennsylvania: Trinity Press International, 1995.

Hyde, Catherine Ryan. *Pay It Forward*. New York: Simon & Schuster, 2010.

Johnson, Elizabeth A. *She Who Is: The Mystery of God in Feminist Theological Discourse*. New York: Crossroad, 1994.

Jones, Peter Rhea. *The Teachings of the Parables*. Nashville: Broadman Press, 1982.

Jung, C. G. *Archetypes and the Collective Unconscious*. B. F. C. Hull, translator. Bollingen Series XX. Princeton University Press, 1969.

_____. *Encountering Jung: On Evil*. Selected and Introduced by Murray Stein. Princeton: Princeton University Press. 1995.

Kaufman, Gordon D. *The Theological Imagination: Constructing the Concept of God*. Philadelphia: Westminster Press, 1981.

_____. *In Face of Mystery: A Constructive Theology*. Cambridge: Harvard University Press, 1993.

_____. *God, Mystery, Diversity*. Minneapolis: Fortress Press, 1996.

Keller, Ernst and Marie-Luise. *Miracles in Dispute*. Trans. Margaret Kohl. Philadelphia: Fortress Press, 1969.

Keltner, Dacher. *Born To Be Good: The Science of a Meaningful Life*. New York: W. W. Norton & Company, 2009.

Malik, Kenan. *The Quest for a Moral Compass: A Global History of Ethics*. Brooklyn, New York: Melville House Publishing, 2014.

Marxsen, Willi. *The Resurrection of Jesus of Nazareth*. Trans. Margaret Kohl. Philadelphia: Fortress Press, 1970.

McFague, Sallie. *Models of God*. Minneapolis: Augsburg Fortress, 1987.

_____. *The Body of God: An Ecological Theology*. Minneapolis: Augsburg Fortress, 1993.

Meier, John P. *A Marginal Jew: Rethinking the Historical Jesus*. 4 vols. New Haven: Yale University Press, 1991-2009.

Moltmann, Juergen. *The Trinity and the Kingdom*. Margaret Kohl, trans. San Francisco: Harper & Row, 1981.

Moule, C. F. D. ed. *Miracles*. New York: A. R. Mowbray & Co, LTD, 1965.

Muir, John. *The Story of My Boyhood and Youth*. San Francisco: Sierra Club Books, 1988.

Murphy, R. "An Allusion to Mary in the Apocalypse," Theological Studies, 2:565-73, 1949.

Ogden, Shubert. *The Point of Christology*. San Francisco: Harper & Row, 1982.

Outcalt, Todd. *The Other Jesus: Stories from World Religions*. New York: Rowman & Littlefield, 2014.

Pagels, Elaine. *Revelations: Visions, Prophecy, & Politics in the Book of Revelation*. New York: Penguin Group. 2012.

Pannenberg, Wolfhart. *Jesus-God and Man*. Trans. Lewis L. Wilkins and Duane Priebe. Philadelphia: The Westminster Press, 1968.

Perrin, Norman. *Rediscovering the Teaching of Jesus*. New York: Harper & Row Publishers, 1967.

_____. *The Kingdom of God in the Teaching of Jesus*. Philadelphia: Westminster Press, 1963.

Plato. *The Collected Dialogues of Plato Including the Letters*. Trans. Lane Cooper et al. Edited by Edith Hamilton and Huntington Cairns. Princeton: Princeton Press, 1961.

Richardson, Cyril C. *The Doctrine of the Trinity*. Nashville: Abingdon Press, 1958.

Rohde, Joachim. *Rediscovering the Teaching of the Evangelists*. Trans. Dorothea M. Barton. Philadelphia: The Westminster Press, 1968.

Ruti, Mari. *The Summons of Love*. New York: Columbia University Press, 2011.

Schleiermacher, Friedrich. *On Religion: Speeches to Its Cultured Despisers*. New York: Harper & Row, 1958.

_____. *The Christian Faith*. Trans. H. R. MacKintosh and J. S. Stewart. 2 Vols. New York: Harper & Row, 1963.

Schurer, Emil. *A History of the Jewish People in the Time of Jesus Christ*. 3 vols. Edinburg: T & T Clark, 1890.

Schweitzer, Albert. *Reverence for Life*. New York: Pilgrim Press, 1969.

_____. *The Quest for the Historical Jesus*. Trans. W. Montgomery. New York: Macmillan Publishing Co. 1968.

Selhub, Eva M. *The Love Response*. New York: Ballantine Books, 2009.

Stagg, Frank. *The Holy Spirit Today*. Nashville: Broadman Press, 1973.

Stein, Robert H. *The Method and Message of Jesus' Teaching*. Revised Edition. Louisville: Westminster John Knox Press, 1994.

_____. *An Introduction to the Parables of Jesus*. Philadelphia: Westminster Press, 1981.

Suchocki, Marjorie Hewitt. *God Christ Church: A Practical Guide to Process Theology*. New Revised Edition. New York: The Crossroad Publishing Company, 1989.

_____. *The End of Evil: Process Eschatology in Historical Context*. Albany: State University, 1988.

_____. *in God's Presence: Theological Reflections on Prayer*. St. Louis: Chalice Press, 1996.

Taylor, Shelley E. *The Tending Instinct*. New York: Henry Holt, 2002.

The Greek New Testament, Ed. Kurt Aland, Matthew Black, Carlo M. Martini, Bruce Metzger, and Allen Wikgren. Third Edition. United Bible Societies, 1975.

Thompson, Leonard L. *The Book of Revelation: Apocalypse and Empire*. New York: Oxford University Press. 1990.

Tobin, Thomas. "Logos," *The Anchor Bible Dictionary*, Vol. 4. New York: Doubleday, 1992.

Weinberg, Steven. *The First Three Minutes: A Modern View of the Origin of the Universe*. Updated edition. New York: Basic Books, 1988.

Whitehead, Alfred North. *Adventures of Ideas*. New York: The Free Press, 1967.

_____. *Process and Reality*. Corrected Edition, ed. David Ray Griffin and Donald W. Sherburne. New York: The Free Press, 1978.

_____. *Modes of Thought*. New York: The Free Press, 1968.

Wilson, E. O. *Biophilia*. Cambridge: Harvard University Press, 1984.

_____. *The Future of Life*. Washington, D.C.: Island Press, 1994.

Wink, Walter, Engaging *the Powers: Discernment and Resistance in a World of Domination*. Minneapolis: Fortress Press, 1992.

_____. *Naming the Powers: The Language of Power in the New Testament*. Philadelphia: Fortress Press, 1984.

_____. *Unmasking the Powers: The Invisible Forces that Determine Human Existence*. Philadelphia: Fortress Press, 1986.

Wright, N. T. *How God Became King: Getting to the Heart of the Gospels*. London: SPCK, 2011.